D1600642

CHEMICAL ECSTASY

CHEMICAL ECSTASY

PSYCHEDELIC DRUGS AND RELIGION

by WALTER HOUSTON CLARK

Sheed and Ward: New York

Preface

Since 1961, when I had the opportunity to attend seminars organized by Dr. Timothy Leary, then at Harvard, I have invested the bulk of my research energies to the systematic study of the significance of the psychedelic drugs to religion. During this time I have observed or helped to "guide" some 175 administrations of psilocybin and LSD. I have informally questioned about 200 persons who have tried these drugs, have canvassed nearly 100 persons through questionnaire and 50 persons through questionnaire and interview. The "trips" involved included both the legal and the illegal, though my direct contacts were mostly through properly sponsored experiments. I have tried both LSD and psilocybin several times myself. Though primarily focused on religious aspects, my concerns included all properties of the drugs.

Critics of the drugs rightly maintain that reactions are varying and unpredictable. They are as unpredictable as human nature in its manifold complexities, both conscious and unconscious. But my research indicates one steady predictability that one can make with about 99 percent accuracy: Those who look back on their psychedelic journeys from any sort of perspective will be glad that they took the drugs. A strange finding for substances whose dangers have been so highly publicized by many of the most respected members of the scientific and medical communities! There *are* dangers, but the warnings have largely come from those who have seldom, if ever, observed an administration from the beginning to end, have not followed up a *random sample* of psychedelic pilgrims and, above all, *have never tried the drugs*

v

themselves. They have been content with scientific hearsay; they have refused to look through Galileo's telescope!

I make the latter comparison advisedly, for, if preliminary findings can be substantiated, a breakthrough in certain very resistant types of mental illness is around the corner. Furthermore, such successes are closely bound up with the religious properties of the drugs, an aspect often neglected even by knowledgeable researchers. In addition, the drugs provide the most ready access to what William James declared was the root of religion, namely mystical experience, the most captivating and transforming experience known to man. I do not say categorically that the discovery of LSD ranks with the Copernican revolution; only that it might. Much patient, open-minded, critical research remains to be done before we will know the value of the drugs either for science or for religion. In the meantime, it is to be hoped that the law will recognize the constitutional right of citizens so disposed to use the drugs under sacramental and carefully controlled conditions in order to gather the evidence to test these chemicals' value for religion and for society. It is an amazing experience to observe the development of compassion and gentleness as one effect of the psychedelic drugs. Loren Eiseley has written, "The need is not really for more brains, the need is now for a gentler, more tolerant people than those who won for us against the ice, the tiger and the bear."* If indeed it *is* understanding, empathy, and compassion of which our generation stands in such dire need, then only a timid compulsion to seek the safety of the herd will turn scholars away from the lessons a resolute investigation of these powerful drugs will offer.

In my eight-year study of the psychedelics I have made a conscientious effort to weigh properly all aspects of the problem. I have tried to put myself as well as I could in the position of those I now criticize, and I think I can say that, at one time or another,

* *The Immense Journey* (New York: Vintage Books, 1957), p. 144.

my emotions and tentative opinions have reflected to some degree all of the alarms that have been sounded. But I have tried to search out and sift the evidence, always preferring that which firsthand observation has offered to me when that was available.

Particularly with the Harvard incident, with which I was in close contact, I have tried to identify with the Harvard authorities. The result has been that at least I have sympathized with their dilemmas, and I am glad not to have been in their positions at the time of the Leary controversy. Yet I must say that my research, almost from the very beginning, has pointed toward the rightness of Dr. Leary and the error of his critics at Harvard, as my pages will document.

I have tried to present my subject clearly and simply so as to instruct not only the specialist in religion and psychology but the generally educated reader as well. In any case, in the early stages of any scientific approach to a subject it is necessary to describe the field, which I try to do in appropriate sections. I have not essayed the awesome task of tracing the infinite complexities of inner space, leaving that to the successors of Freud, Rank and Jung, as well as to the theologians. I have simply tried to describe my own observations and the reports of others, attempting to sharpen the reader's emotional perceptions when empathic involvement is important to understanding. This I do chiefly by citing cases and quotations from subjects. In other words, I have concentrated on descriptions of the phenomena.

I like to reflect that parts of the book have been written in many places: not only in my attic study at Newton Centre and in my summer study in the woods of Wolfeboro, New Hampshire, but also snatches in the beautiful city library in the civic center of Tulsa, Oklahoma, at the busy Kansas City airport, flying over the Rockies after my visit to the coast area of California and circling the blue waters surrounding Istanbul.

My thanks are due, first of all, to my wife Ruth, who, because she disapproves of all drugs, has acted the part of a kind of *particeps criminis* in encouraging my research, spurring me to a faithful adherence to my writing schedule, protecting me from interruptions and dispensing with my company when work on certain aspects of the project called me away from home. My friend Timothy Leary introduced me to the psychedelic chemicals and so to an interest that has proved so absorbing and so enlightening to me. It has multiplied my insights into the psychology of religion, and so has enabled me to deepen my lifelong interest in religious experience to an extent, which only a few years ago would have been to me unbelievable.

Dr. Dana Farnsworth, Professor David McClelland and the late Professor Gordon Allport in particular spent time to help me understand the point of view of members of the Harvard community relative to the Leary affair. Very helpful to me during my visit to California were Dr. Joel Fort, Dr. David Smith, Dolores Craton and other members of the Haight-Ashbury Medical Clinic and Mr. and Mrs. Emmett Tolman and their daughter Felicia of Laguna Beach. I owe many insights to Dr. Walter N. Pahnke, Dr. Stanislav Grof, Mr. William Richard and other friends on the staff of the Maryland Psychiatric Research Center; also to my colleagues in experiments at Norwich Hospital, Connecticut under government grants held by the Worcester Foundation for Experimental Biology and Clark University: Drs. John Bergen, Werner Koella, Donald Krus and Milton Raskin.

Background information on the experiments at the Massachusetts Correctional Institution at Concord was secured through the generous cooperation of volunteers, especially Messrs. Donald M. Painten, John Kerrigan, Gerard Alliette and other members of the Self Development Group there; also from members of the staff, in particular the late Edward Grennan, Superintendent; Vincent Rice, Director of Treatment; and Lieutenant Victor Pozericki. Members of the United Illuminating Company Community at Fort Hill, Roxbury, Massachusetts, have been hospitable and helpful in the exchange of views on the occasion of several visits. Former colleagues who have especially encouraged me in my research and enriched me with their insights include President Emeritus Herbert Gezork and Professor Meredith Handspicker of Andover Newton Theological School and Professors Culbert G. Rutenber and Norman K. Gottwald, now of California Baptist Theological Seminary.

Among those who have helped me through an exchange of views or more substantially I should mention Dr. Bernard Aaronson of the New Jersey Neuropsychiatric Institute, Dr. G. W. Arendsen Hein, Medical Director of Foundation Stichting, Veluweland Hospital, Ederveen, Holland; Dr. Clemens Benda, Miss Lisa Bieberman, the Rev. Betty A. Bogert of the United Church of Christ, Dr. Leo Cass of Harvard University Health Services, my son Professor Jonathan Clark of Boston University, Dr. Joseph Havens of the Health Services of the University of Massachusetts, Professor Karl Kiralis of the University of Houston, the Rev. Arthur Kleps of the Neo-American Church, Dr. Stanley Krippner of Maimonides Hospital, Brooklyn, New York; Mrs. J. D. Kuch of the Neo-American Church, Dr. Hanscarl Leuner, Head of the Psychotherapeutic Department, University of Gottingen; Dr. Herman Lisco of Harvard Medical School, Dr. William H. McGlothlin of University of Southern California, Mr. Malcolm Margolin, Mr. Donald Mead, the late Dr. Max Rinkel, Rabbi Zalman Schachter, Professor Huston Smith of Massachusetts Institute of Technology, Professor Richard Underwood of Hartford Seminary, Miss Mary Wicks, Probation Officer, Kidderminster, Worcester, England; Dr. John W. Aiken and Dr. Louisa Aiden, founders of the Church of the Awakening; and many other persons too numerous to mention.

Miss B. L. Harte was my chief and invaluable secretarial and editorial assistant. Secretarial help has also been given by Mrs. J. Clement McCann and Mr. Warren Prescott.

Contents

CHEMICAL ECSTASY

1. Psychological Models

By the continual living activity of its nonrational elements a religion is guarded from passing into 'rationalism.' By being steeped in and saturated with rational elements it is guarded from sinking into fanaticism or mere mysticality, or at least from persisting in these, and is qualified to become a religion for all civilized humanity. The degree in which both rational and nonrational elements are jointly present, united in healthy and lovely harmony, affords a criterion to measure the relative rank of religions—and one, too, that is specifically religious.

—Rudolf Otto[1]

Seven years ago a thirty-six-year-old bank robber serving a twenty-year sentence in a state prison was given a psychedelic drug. The result was a vision of Christ in which this hardened, cynical and unbelieving man participated vividly in the drama of the crucifixion. Profoundly shaken, he stared out the hospital window of the prison where the experiment was taking place. "All my life came before my eyes," he told me, "and I said to myself, what a waste!" The drug has not automatically solved all of his problems, but now they have become the problems of rehabilitating himself and rejoining society. I have asked him to recount his vision several times, a moving experience both for him and his hearers. Without exception, the latter are impressed with his gentleness and compassion. Prison officials who knew him before consider him reformed. Certainly, in his aims and values, he has been radically changed. He and other convicts participating in the experiment have founded an organization to

3

rehabilitate themselves and their fellows. Without his dedication, the project might have failed several times.

A young woman, a mathematics graduate from a top women's college and an argumentative atheist, is given morning glory seeds. As a result, she recognizes her need for God and her profound impulse toward a way of life that is basically religious, and she becomes actively involved as a member of the Society of Friends. Disturbed by what she sees as the irresponsibility of many of those who use the psychedelics, she has dedicated herself to the task of circulating reliable information about the drugs and to founding a retreat where these drugs may be used in appropriate surroundings under experienced guides. One point of difference with some highly visible cultists is that she sees no need to look toward Hinduism and Buddhism for a framework for the psychedelic drug experience. Her keen and highly articulate logical faculties have now found a religious thrust within the tradition of Christian mysticism, which would have been incredible to her during most of her high school and college years.

In another experiment an instructor in theology was given psilocybin, the "mushroom drug." An excellent teacher, his students particularly commented on the effectiveness of his lectures on death. In the middle of the experiment he approached the supervising physician in great distress. "Wally," he exclaimed, "give me the antidote! I am dying!" But the doctor was psychiatrist enough to know that the drug had unearthed a basic problem which he needed to face sooner or later. So he gave him a placebo. By the time he realized that the experience had not been aborted, he felt only gratitude toward the physician, because he had faced the experience and come to terms with it. Following his experience, he was riding on a public conveyance. Suddenly he looked around at the faces of the people in the car and seemed to know them with a depth of feeling usually reserved for his immediate family. He seemed to experience directly his brotherhood with all of mankind.

Skeptical readers will be disposed to dismiss these examples as too extreme and highly colored. Those who have used the stronger psychedelic drugs probably will not. I have selected them because they illustrate the theme of this volume, the religious aspects of the psychedelic drugs. Not everyone who uses the drugs will discover religion, but experiences like these are by no means uncommon. They occur in many types and classes of subjects under widely differing conditions. Protestants, Catholics, Jews, and also those of no traditional faith, have encountered the religious dimensions of the psychedelics. The convict did not even know in what religious tradition he had been brought up and had volunteered mainly to impress the parole board. The interested reader can find similar illustrations in other volumes.[2]

But if cases like the above can be cited in favor of a clear link between the psychedelics and religion, does this mean that we have a ready tool at hand for intensifying religion and making it more effective? Anyone with any knowledge of the field at all knows that the situation is more complicated than this. My eye runs over a clipping from the *New York Times* of May 2, 1968, with the headline "Woman LSD User Commits Suicide." The tragic story tells of a thirty-five-year-old woman so anxious that others have as beneficial an experience as hers that she had been distributing LSD to others, once to a Yale student who severely injured himself when he jumped from the window of a motel during intoxication. Facing a possible sentence of ten years in prison for her good intentions, the woman chose death instead.

Obviously, the drugs have their seamy side, and the situation is complex. I propose to study the religious aspects of the psychedelic drugs in this volume, to throw what light I can on religion from an examination of drug experiences, to point out some major complexities, to recount some of the pertinent history of the drug movement and to balance the bad against the good.

What Is Religion? "Religion" is one of the most elusive terms in the language. Any unabridged dictionary will list a dozen or more definitions. These can be multiplied by the addition of many more by anyone who wishes to collect them from his friends or even from various experts in the study of religious fields. Religion is one of the richest and most complex functions of the individual and of society. Hence, it will be necessary for me to give the reader at least a general idea of what I will have in mind when I use the term, "religion," in this volume.

In the first place, I will not have in mind the social or institutional aspects of religion as much as religion in its personal forms. I will be speaking of religious experience, and whether or not it can be associated with the use of the psychedelic drugs. *Religion,* I will be thinking of as *the inner experience of the individual when he senses Ultimate Reality,* whether as God, a Beyond, transcendent cosmic process, a wholly different and profound dimension of life, Nirvana, or however one chooses to name and interpret this ultimate reality, and *particularly when this experience is confirmed by the attempts of the individual to harmonize his life with the Reality he senses.* This definition leans in the direction of mystical forms of consciousness, though it does not require them. It also implies some consequences of the experience, preferably in a form which can be observed by other people, but it does not absolutely require this. Some consequences are so subtle and so intimate that only the one who experiences them can be sensible of them. It would be hard to imagine any religious experience that had no consequences at all, even though the experience were very superficial and the consequences slight. However, since one of the evidences on which we rely is what the subject tells us of this inner experience, it is possible for us to be mistaken and infer that there had been religious experience when actually the individual is merely using religious language. Pious words are highly valued in certain social groups, and individuals may develop considerable skill in varnishing their public images with words of sanctity. For this reason, the student of religious experience must be on his guard against a too eager readiness to accept mere words as evidences of religious experience. He must be alert to look for other indicators of genuineness and depth. "By their fruits ye shall know them."

Religion and Drugs

The association of drugs with religious experience is so offensive to some that they will deny that such things can be. Of course, some may wish to define experiences in which drugs play a part as *ipso facto* nonreligious. To do so is to beg the whole question. A common criticism has it that whatever is touched off by the psychedelic drugs can only be "pseudo-religion," a religious hoax or fake. Such assertions do not usually make clear just what their definition of religion is, but their denial that religion can be drug-involved is implicit. There are many for whom the idea that religion can in any way come from drugs is too new to adjust to readily, though they have no objection to such artificialities as fasting, organ music, liturgy or prolonged periods of meditation. Adults often feel that young people should be discouraged from using drugs, unless they are disguised as cigarettes or beverages. They feel that if they acknowledge that drugs might trigger religion, they will accord drugs more dignity and glamor than is prudent. I consider such tactics, in the long run, bad strategy. Even though benevolent, distortion backfires. But it should be noted that I have made no exclusion of drugs in my definition of religion. In this and subsequent chapters I hope to make it clear why I believe that drugs, under certain circumstances, may be *a factor* of some importance in many cases of religious experience, even though never the chief factor. Indeed, I could say *always* a factor if we could admit as "drugs" those powerful biochemicals, more often called hormones, which are natural in the human body and without whose involvement no act of human consciousness, sacred or profane, can occur.

Rational vs. Nonrational Religion

Religion is a complex function, and though I believe that religious experience is the human core of religion, it certainly does not constitute all of it. When someone who has had a religious experience attempts to harmonize his life with the Reality that he senses, his effort goes beyond the experience and may eventuate in many more or less successful attempts to further his search for perfect harmony. To attempt a full account of this religious search would take us far beyond the proposed confines of this limited volume, but I might generalize two main types of psychological activities, with differing functions, that apply to all religion. I am speaking very generally of the rational and the nonrational activities or functions of the human mind.

When I speak of the nonrational, it is important to make the point that I do *not* mean the irrational, though nonrational experience sometimes may degenerate into the irrational. Listening to a symphony for most people is probably not a rational experience, for its delights derive from nonrational sources, yet attending a concert is not irrational. Esthetic experience of any kind is primarily nonrational, and the same can be said for religious experience.

In western religion, as in western culture generally, the tendency has been to emphasize the rational and to neglect the nonrational. That certain benefits have accrued to the West from this tradition is clear. Science, the chief flower of the rational intellect, along with its attendant technology, exploited through an aggressive activism, has given the West certain advantages over the East with its relatively greater valuation of the esthetic life, relaxation and passivity. In similar fashion, western religions, in particular the Catholic Church of the Middle Ages, opted for an Aristotelian world view and logic that characterized not only scholastic theology but has dominated most forms of Catholic, Protestant, Jewish and Mohammedan theology since that day. Wedded to a gospel of righteousness with its roots in the Jewish prophetic tradition, this combination of rationality and the concept of righteousness has led to modern movements of social justice for which western society owes a large debt, directly and indirectly, to the churches. Contemporary movements in pursuit of civil rights in twentieth century America are cases in point. Contrasted with the record of most eastern religions in this respect, the western religions seem plainly superior.

But there has been a progressive weakening of the religious dynamic in these same movements and a consequent loss of the religious vigor from which the movements might have profited, because western religion neglected the hunger for the expression of the nonrational. This has not been the case in the East. But there is something in the charge that eastern faiths have emphasized meditation and the delights of mystical withdrawal from the world to the exclusion of social justice and the practical alleviation of human suffering. It seems clear that students of comparative religion are on sound ground when they advocate a religious dialogue between the East and the West. It will help us to understand these practical and social aspects of our religious culture and also the dynamics of the religious life, if we consider the relation of the rational and nonrational components of the religious consciousness. Furthermore, it will throw light on the type of consciousness mediated by the psychedelic drugs and will help to explain why those whose experience with the drugs is religious tend to interpret their experiences in the terms of eastern rather than western concepts. Western theology has tended to be out of touch with the mystical roots of religious experience.

As I have already suggested, the religious consciousness is governed equally by rational and nonrational functions. The function of the nonrational element is to awaken and to vitalize the religious sense, to give it color, vigor and motivation. The nonrational mediates a firsthand perception of the Holy and the individual's relation to it. This nonrational and immediate perception is usually accompanied by emotion, excitement and feeling, though the feeling is a concomitant of the nonrational rather than its essential principle. The function of the rational, on the other hand, is to guide, criticize and conceptualize the nonrational. Religion dominated by the nonrational may get out of hand, either through an indulgent cultivation of a captivating experience, which leads to a selfish withdrawal from social obligations, or to a fanatical interference with the lives of others, which may lead to social strife and chaos. Rational religion, on the other hand, may become desiccated, bland and formal, because words, concepts and institutions usurp the place of warmth and compassion. Ideally, these two functions should work in balance to achieve an intuitive perfection. Unfortunately, however, this perfection is found no more often in practice than is any other ideal.

In *The Idea of the Holy*, Rudolf Otto has compared religion to a piece of cloth with the nonrational composing the warp and the rational the woof, no cloth being possible with warp or woof alone. Other thinkers such as Schleiermacher, Bergson, and, perhaps, Spinoza have referred to the nonrational element in religion, calling it variously *feeling, intuition, instinct* or something else. A more dynamic figure of the relationship between the rational and the nonrational is that of the function of the rudder and the wind in a sailing ship. To bring this up-to-date, we can refer to the motor ship with a rudder and an engine, the nonrational being the engine and reason the rudder. No matter how perfectly the rudder functions, the ship will get nowhere. With a powerful engine alone, the ship may be a hazard to itself and to other navigation.

In the West the rudder of reason and the rational has received the emphasis. Lacking warmth and drive, many churches and religions have either passed out of existence or have continued in a kind of institutional living death. Such vigor as their individual members have derives from secular sources unrelated to any profound spiritual motives. Those whose interests impel them to defend this kind of religion point to the mischief caused by the emotionalism generated in fanatical sects. Their nonrational energy, like the wind, blows them where it wills. Ideally, the happy result of a combination of the two is the safe arrival of the ship at the port of personality integration, cosmic purpose and social righteousness.

Drugs and Mysticism

Of the two functions, the nonrational is more usually stimulated by the psychedelic experience. Frequently it makes its appearance in perceptions of a mystical nature that may present themselves in a variety of symbolic forms. As the mystics so often have asserted, the mystical consciousness is ineffable, and its comparative neglect by western religions has resulted in the vocabularies of eastern faiths being much richer and more precise in this area, hence more useful to the mystic. Furthermore, western theologians have been more suspicious of the mystics, whose poetic phrases often wreak havoc with the dogmas and logical systems so dear to the theological mind. Perhaps this confrontation of the mystic by the theologian has been nowhere so sharp as with the issue of Pantheism, considered heresy in practically all branches of the Christian Church and in Judaism and Mohammedanism as well. It was for the heresy of Pantheism that one of the greatest of all Christian mystics, the Dominican Meister Eckhart, was condemned in the fourteeenth century.

In the mystical experience the subject feels himself one with the cosmos, which to him may be the equivalent of God. Thus, unless he watches his language very carefully, he may give others the impression that he thinks he *is* God, with the consequences of arrogance, dogmatism and self-worship, which may lead others astray. I do not know any study which demonstrates that this is the actual practice of Pantheists outside the theological area. W. T. Stace suggests that the problem may in large part be a semantic one to be solved by a proper understanding of the role of paradox in the language of the mystics.[3] God may be at once *both* immanent and transcendent. The mystic may feel at the same time one with God and infinitely separated from Him. Whatever the problem in the western tradition, there is no doubt that eastern theologians have been much more hospitable to the mystical consciousness, and this helps us to understand the preference that many drug takers have for eastern modes of conceptualization and practice. There are sound reasons for preferring the western tradition, at least for westerners. We will return to this in a later chapter.

I would like to complete this introduction with a few words about the importance of mystical religion. William James has said that "personal religious experience has its root and centre in mystical states of consciousness."[4] To the extent, then, that the student of religion sees religious experience as an essential element in effective religion, he will be interested in the mystical consciousness and anything that will enhance it or throw light on it.

The claim that the psychedelic drugs enhance mysticism provides the chief reason for this book. There has been a sort of unwritten conspiracy on the part of "respectable" society, and even science, to suppress this facet of psychedelic drug phenomena, along with other of their favorable aspects.

I will first attempt to examine critically their religious potentialities in order to discuss both their usefulness and danger to the religious life. I will also say something of the values, as well as the dangers, of drug-induced religion. In preparation for this, I will present a chapter of cases to give the reader some idea of the variety of religious phenomenon induced by these drugs, some of them carefully studied by myself. Following this, I will devote some space to the history of the psychedelic drug movement, particularly in the United States. These materials will provide a background against which the religious values of the drugs may be weighed, this forming the main focus of the book.

NOTES

1. Rudolf Otto, *The Idea of the Holy* (New York: Oxford University Press, 1958), pp. 141-142.
2. See the chapter on religious and mystical experience in R. E. L. Masters and J. Houston, *The Varieties of Psychedelic Experience* (New York: Holt, Rinehart & Winston, 1966), and cases in which a variety of persons describe their "trips" in R. Metzner, ed., *The Ecstatic Adventure* (New York: Macmillan, 1968).
3. W. T. Stace, *Mysticism and Philosophy* (Philadelphia: Lippincott, 1960), chap. 4.
4. William James, *The Varieties of Religious Experience* (New York: New American Library, 1958), p. 292.

2. A Chapter of Cases: Non-Drug-Induced

What is that which gleams through me and smites my heart without wounding it? I am both a-shudder and a-glow.
—St. Augustine

The ecstatic experience of a mystical nature is probably the most captivating and moving, though it may be also the most frightening and awesome, experience known to man. It is also the most thoroughly transforming and the most enlightening of all human experience. More than any one single facet of religion, it constitutes the psychological foundation on which the whole enterprise known as "religion" is built. It is the ultimate source from which the strength of religion flows, even though this foundation and this source may become a faraway, dried and broken memory lost among the ruins of countless institutions whose directors sought power and security instead of God; who became tyrannical on the one hand or bland and harmless on the other.

It is this power of religious ecstasy to "give freedom to the captives," that has made it so sought after, whether as the "pearl of great price" of the Christian or the Nirvana of the Buddhist. Plato was doubtless thinking of Socrates' night of enlightenment before Potidea when he composed the famous Allegory of the Cave in the seventh chapter of *The Republic* and put it into the mouth of Socrates. He who has been surprised by the ecstatic moment immediately recognizes the language of those who speak

14

of "death and rebirth." He understands the words of Jesus when He told the bewildered Nicodemus that in order to see salvation he must be "born again."

How do ecstatics describe their experiences? How do they convey its essence to others? The answer is that they do not convey its essence to any except those who have had similar experience themselves, whether under a drug or not. Even the most colorful and passionate words seem inaccurate and pale. It is this paleness and insufficiency of language of which the mystics down the centuries have complained. They have talked and talked, like the Ancient Mariner compelled to tell his tale, whether people have understood them or not. They have always complained that words are not enough, and they have manufactured allegories and poetic figures in a kind of broken and stuttering beauty born of longing and frustration. I will supply first a few traditional examples of ecstasy triggered by no drug, and then other cases in which I will indicate as well as I can what the drug experience seems like to the inward consciousness of those who have ingested drugs that have triggered a firsthand awareness of the religious consciousness.

SOME CLASSICAL ECSTASIES

Isaiah

The first of these examples might well have constituted the protocol of a report on his LSD experience by the subject of a modern experiment. It is the vision of the cherubim seen by Isaiah, found in the sixth chapter of his Prophecy. I present it in the stately cadences of the King James' English.

THE VISION AND CALL OF ISAIAH

In the year that King Uzziah died I saw also the Lord sitting upon a throne, high and lifted up, and his train filled the temple.

Above it stood the seraphims: each one had six wings; with twain he
covered his face, and with twain he covered his feet, and with twain
he did fly.

And one cried unto another, and said, Holy, holy, holy, is the Lord of
hosts: the whole earth is full of his glory.

And the posts of the door moved at the voice of him that cried, and
the house was filled with smoke.

Then said I, Woe is me! for I am undone; because I am a man of
unclean lips, and I dwell in the midst of people of unclean lips: for
mine eyes have seen the King, the Lord of hosts.

Then flew one of the seraphims unto me, having a live coal in his hand,
which he had taken with the tongs from off the altar:

And he laid it upon my mouth, and said Lo, this hath touched thy
lips; and thine iniquity is taken away, and thy sin purged.

Also I heard the voice of the Lord, saying, Whom shall I send, and
who will go for us? Then said I, Here am I; send me (Is. 6:1-8).

This ecstasy beautifully illustrates our definition of religion,
combining, as it does, Isaiah's sensing of the Ultimate in his
vision of the Lord, and the attempt in the last verse to harmonize
his life with the reality he has sensed in his response to the call.
It initiated his ministry of social righteousness. It also resembles
what we often encounter in reports of those who have taken the
psychedelic drugs in its highly symbolic description of what, in
the last analysis, is unutterable.

Pascal's Night of Ecstasy

The next example is Blaise Pascal's famous description of the
ecstasy that so shook him that he wrote it down and sewed it
up in his coat, where it was found after his death. For some

reason, mathematicians like Kepler, Newton and Einstein often show mystical tendencies, and Pascal was one of the great mathematical and scientific geniuses of western culture. Here we see one of the masters of clear French prose reduced to a few broken phrases trying to describe the key experience of his life:

PASCAL'S MYSTIC AMULET

The year of grace 1654, 23 November
From about half-past ten in the evening
until about half-past twelve, midnight.

FIRE.

God of Abraham, God of Isaac, God of Jacob.
Not of the philosophers nor of the wise.
Assurance, joy, assurance, feeling, joy, peace.

GOD OF JESUS CHRIST;
My God and thy God.
Thy God shall be my God.

Forgotten of the world and of all except God;
He is only found in the ways taught in the Gospel,

THE SUBLIMITY OF THE HUMAN SOUL.

Father, the world has not known thee, but I have known thee.
Joy, joy, joy, tears of joy.
I do not separate myself from thee.

They left me behind, me a fountain of living water.
My God do not leave me. . . .

JESUS CHRIST—JESUS CHRIST.

I have separated myself from him;
I have fled, renounced, crucified him. . . .

RECONCILIATION TOTAL AND SWEET.

Total submission to JESUS CHRIST and to my DIRECTOR. . . .
Amen.[1]

Apparently, the amulet or memorial was a collection of notes hastily written down to remind himself of this evening of ecstasy and awe. Unlike Isaiah's account, Pascal's descriptive phrases are confined to the one word, "FIRE." This is a common feature in many ecstasies. It is sometimes used figuratively, but often it is used almost literally, in terms of the inward consciousness of the ecstatic. The rest of the passage describes the intensity of the feeling that has been released and its resolution. The date marked an abrupt change in Pascal's interests and emphases.

The Mysticism of Jan van Ruysbroeck

Jan van Ruysbroeck was a fourteenth century Dutch mystic. Since the ecstatic of any kind is unable to describe his experience with anything approaching scientific precision, he is often forced to use figures of speech, allegories and riddles, often of a paradoxical nature. Consequently, he becomes the poet of the religious life. Because few mystics were more gifted poetically than van Ruysbroeck, his writing is very beautiful and moving. The central feature of all mysticism is not an emotion but a very vivid perception of an undifferentiated unity underlying, not merely the world, but the total cosmos. In Christianity this is usually identified as God, and sometimes referred to as "the void," the "dark silence," the "Abyss," or by a similar suggestive concept.

The following is part of one of van Ruysbroeck's best-known passages, though it is only a fragment of a complete experience:

For in this unfathomable abyss of the Simplicity, all things are wrapped in fruitive bliss; and the abyss itself may not be comprehended, unless by the Essential Unity. To this the persons and all that lives in God, must give place; for here there is nought else but an eternal rest in the fruitive embrace of an outpouring Love. And this is that wayless being which all interior spirits have chosen above all other things. This is the dark silence in which all lovers lose themselves. But if we would prepare ourselves for it by means of the virtues, we should strip ourselves of all but our very bodies, and should flee forth into the wild Sea, whence no created thing can draw us back again.[2]

It is hardly theology to refer to God as "the dark silence in which all lovers lose themselves," or the "wild Sea" into which we would flee, but these moving and suggestive phrases open windows of perceptive feeling and enrich the understanding of God even for the commonplace seeker. It is similar eloquence, born of ecstasy, that one finds again and again in the protocols of those striving to describe their drug experiences.

A Modern Mystic. Though not as highly prized as in former times, mysticism is common in the present day—much more common than is generally realized; for sometimes mystics themselves misunderstand their ecstasies as pathology or as something so unusual that no one could comprehend them. Even clergymen, who are usually taught to approach religion rationally, are puzzled.

The following description comes from a woman who came to me for counseling. Forty-five years old, she had held a comfortable berth as a professor in a university. Brought up fairly nonreligiously and trained in science, the experience had overwhelmed her and completely changed her values. She reminds one of Pascal. Here are her notes:

1. Timelessness,
2. Spacelessness,
3. Deep quiet—vibrant—not excitement,
4. Described better by what it is *not*; not sleep, a dream, daydreaming, saw or heard nothing, yet all coming from outside;
5. I was not there nor anywhere in this familiar world, but definitely being. I was as a being—almost formless. Time dropped out but invaded all.

6. It was another world: magnificent, vibrant, joyous, dynamic—*More*. There was moreness—not different from this world but more. I was in it, through it, participating in it—not an observer. This awareness was sudden, yet timeless. This other realm was very *real*—not a glimpse, but the whole of it was there. Did not want to possess it, or reject or love—no feeling *toward* it, but *in* all being. Too close to respond or react to it, but *in* it.

7. Afterwards: agonizing loneliness. Could not give it, explain it, share it, yet it *had* to be shared, given. Felt a part of all mankind—suffered intensely with people—loved them within themselves. Yet was separated from them. They could not receive what I wanted to give.

8. Love, power, truth, Christ, God intensely real.

Afterward she found an enhanced ability to relate to people and a heightened interest in religion. Later she resigned her position in order to study theology. A friend of long standing testified that she had changed from the self-centered, thoughtless, inconsiderate person she had once been. Yet she also increased in her ability to suffer, and her changed position brought her many problems. In the midst of her problems she was asked whether she wished she had never had her experience. Without a moment's hesitation, she declared, "I would rather die than be the person I was before!"

These cases of naturally occurring religious ecstasy will serve as a brief background in this area. Though they hardly do justice to the variety of individual experience, they will give the reader a preliminary "feel" for the area. This should be at least one means of testing intuitively the similarity or lack of similarity of drug-induced ecstasy to more traditional forms of religious experience. I would like to introduce a few scriptural cases of a more violent and frightening type, which occasionally suggest what today would be labeled as mental illness.

ECSTASIES OF FEAR AND TERROR

These four cases have been consistent in that they represent positive ecstatic experiences. All contain suggestions of great power, ratified by the changed character of the lives of the subjects. Most of us, even though we may deplore our sins and wholly disapprove of some of our habits, nevertheless find our wills unequal to the task of mending our ways and at the same time of retaining the tranquil, spontaneous, yet effective, disposition that we covet. As the cases demonstrate, it is the power often born of religious ecstasy that can make the changed life possible.

This power is not easily won, and ecstasy may on occasion produce little more than struggle, fear and chaos. It is true, as Nietzsche reminds us, that it may require chaos to produce the "dancing star," but the ecstatic nature may also descend into madness, as the example of King Saul in the Bible reminds us. Physicians have a general principle that any medicine strong enough to cure is strong enough to be abused. Even table salt may kill.

And so the note of power and strength sounded in most accounts of religious ecstasy gives rise to what Rudolf Otto terms the sense of the *numinous* and the *mysterium tremendum,* or *the mystery that makes one tremble.*[3] This element makes not only the conventional religious person but also many theologians a little wary when they consider religion in its nonrational and ecstatic forms. As Scripture reminds us, it is indeed "a fearful thing to fall into the hands of the living God" (Heb. 10:31).

Psychologically, we can partially explain this feature of ecstatic religion by stating that the levels of the psyche that must be activated for the encounter with God are also those containing primitive impulses of great power, not to speak of the vials of wrath and madness that threaten to unseat the reason. In biblical, medieval, and even modern times, this has been known as "possession by devils." The dynamics are best described for us today in the pages of A. T. Boisen and C. G. Jung.[4]

William James discusses this issue in the first chapter of his *The Varieties of Religious Experience*, which he concludes in the following colorful and perceptive passage:

As regards the psychopathic origin of so many religious phenomena, that would not be in the least surprising or disconcerting. . . . Few of us are not in some ways infirm, or even diseased; and our very infirmities help us unexpectedly. In the psychopathic temperament we have the emotionality which is the *sine qua non* of moral perception; we have the intensity and tendency to emphasis which are the essence of practical moral vigor; and we have the love of metaphysics and mysticism which carry one's interests beyond the surface of the sensible world. What, then, is more natural than that this temperament should introduce one to regions of religious truth, to corners of the universe, which your robust Philistine type of nervous system, forever offering its biceps to be felt, thumping its breast, and thanking Heaven that it hasn't a single morbid fibre in its composition, would be sure to hide forever from its self-satisfied possessors?

If there were such a thing as inspiration from a higher realm, it might well be that the neurotic temperament would furnish the chief condition of the requisite receptivity.

For "neurotic" we might read "sensitive." It is the sensitive instrument that most easily gets out of kilter.

The experience of the *mysterium tremendum*, the fear of the Lord," "holy terror," or whatever terms are used, is the tribute paid by the creature to the presence of his awesome Creator. "Can a man see God and live?" Can his sanity survive? There are moments when such questions, spoken or unspoken, threaten the peace of every saint and every prophet. For this reason, courage is a requisite for every ecstatic, whether he is submitting to the whirlwind of God's inspiration carrying him he knows not where, or whether he is enduring the finger of warning pointed at him by well-meaning defenders of a conventional faith. Examples of this abound in classical tradition and in modern instances. For illustrative cases we do not need to go beyond the pages of Holy Scripture.

More than a hint of religious awe is found immediately on opening the Bible in the majestic phrases of the account of the Creation in Genesis. Terror is suggested by the wrath of God expressed in the angel with the flaming sword who bars Eden to Adam and Eve and by the punishment of Cain for the murder of his brother. God approaches his favorite, Abraham, while he sleeps amidst "a horror of great darkness" and with awesome visions (Gen. 15:12-17). Even more indicative of fear are some of the experiences of the visionary Jacob, especially when he wrestles with God "until the breaking of the day" and declares, "I have seen God face to face, and my life is preserved" (Gen. 32:24-32).

Perhaps the most famous of the ancient Hebrew ecstatics was Moses. It will be recalled that, having killed an Egyptian for abusing an Israelite, Moses was a fugitive tending sheep in the wilderness near Sinai. Here Moses had his experience before the bush that burned, "and the bush was not consumed" (Ex. 3:2). Subjects under the psychedelics have reported similar experiences.[5]

It is clear that Moses also experienced the *mysterium tremendum,* for "Moses hid his face; for he was afraid to look upon God." This experience emboldened Moses and gave his life purpose. Despite initial reluctance and an encounter with the Lord who "sought to kill him" (Ex. 4:24), Moses led his people out of Egypt. Similar ecstasies, including the ascent of Sinai to receive the Ten Commandments, supported Moses in his labors against obstacles and tribulations throughout the Exodus, ending with his final ecstasy as he glimpsed the promised land from the top of Pisgah (Deut. 34:1). Such was the man "whom the Lord knew face to face . . . in all the great terror which Moses shewed in the sight of all Israel" (Deut. 34:10-12).

A final case is more nebulous, as all these tales from ancient tradition must be. Yet, like the rest, it bears the ring of authentic experiential truth. This is the Book of Job, whose profound truths and vigorous phrases could have issued only from the pen of one who knew ecstasy mingled with the heights of prosperity and the depths of life's tragedy. With the strength which religious ecstasy alone can mediate, Job withstood the orthodoxy of his friends, who sought to comfort him in his grief with contemporary theological platitudes, which his whole soul rejected as error. Looked at in this way, the truths are told through the devices forced on the seer: allegory, symbolism and myth.

The unfolding drama begins with the happiness and prosperity of Job. In all conventional ways he was "perfect and upright . . . one that feared God and eschewed evil." Then through Satan comes a series of works of fearful destruction, ending with the slaughter of all his children and a physical affliction that leaves this proud and righteous man an object of pity. In a fit of righteous fury and with matchless eloquence, Job curses the day he was born and all but curses God, as his wife encourages him to do. His friends, with the self-satisfaction of the orthodox, try to force on him the conviction that he has sinned and so incurred the wrath of the Lord. Though he does not quite know how to combat their strictures, he is convinced that mere words are not sufficient to pierce the heart of the matter.

Throughout, constituting the background of the drama, come the tones of the *tremendum*, the power and fury, the strength and the inscrutable wisdom of an awesome Creator. All of this becomes explicit in the words of the Lord, beginning with Chapter 38 when God, in his wrath, answers Job "out of the whirl-wind," and demands that he "gird up his loins like a man" and answer for his "darkening counsel by words without knowledge." It is here, in the descriptions of the fearfulness and the beauty of nature, the work of God's hands, the cruelty of the ostrich, the keen eye of the eagle as she searches for prey, the "sweet in-fluences of Pleiades," the strength of the proud war-horse as he paws the earth in his longing for battle, the dangers of the fear-some crocodile and the mystery, triumph and terror which the lines convey, that rhetoric in a book of rhetoric reaches its highest peak. It is no wonder that when God finished his creation "the morning stars sang together, and all the sons of God shouted for joy!" (Job 38:7). It is no wonder that a modern ecstatic, like William Blake, who in his own inner experiences encountered all the terrifying beauties of the Book of Job, came closest to an artistic rendering of the spirit of this great Book.

The space is not at hand to carry this theme through the ample pages of world literature. I have provided the reader with a brief glimpse of the depths, the captivating and transforming perceptions and the fearfulness of the experience of God, a true diversity. One can sense why it is that when one properly un-derstands the religious life, it is only the courageous man who is willing to face it. It is necessary to understand all of these facets, of which the foregoing is only a small sampling, if one is to grasp the background that can properly disclose the re-ligious meaning of the psychedelics. To those who say this is nonsense, it is sufficient to ask whether they have been there them-selves, with or without drugs. Then, like Job, they can answer from experiences out of the whirlwind whether we are dealing with forces of infinite good or infinite evil. Paradoxically, they may decide it is something of both. It is hardly likely that they will settle for anything in between.

NOTES

1. Translation in R. M. Bucke, *Cosmic Consciousness* (New Hyde Park, N.Y.: University Books, 1961), pp. 226-227. The statement has been somewhat abridged. Other examples of mysticism and ecstasy will be found in Bucke's volume.
2. Quoted in W. T. Stace, *The Teachings of the Mystics* (New York: New American Library, 1960), p. 169, from van Ruysbroeck's, *The Adornment of the Spiritual Marriage,* trans. C. A. Wynschenck Dom. (London: J. M. Dent and Sons Ltd., 1916).
3. Rudolf Otto, *The Idea of the Holy,* trans. J. W. Harvey (New York: Oxford Univ. Press, 1958), chaps. 2-5.
4. For an account of a highly dramatic conflict between the forces of good and evil set in a context of demonic possession in the times of Richelieu, see Aldous Huxley's, *The Devils of Loudun.*
5. See W. H. Clark in E. P. Booth, ed. *Religion Ponders Science* (New York: Appleton-Century, 1964), chap. 1.

3. A Chapter of Cases: Drug-Induced

But the man who comes back through the Door in the Wall will never be quite the same as the man who went out. He will be wiser but less cocksure, happier but less self-satisfied, humbler in acknowledging his ignorance, yet better equipped to understand the relationship of words to things, of systematic reasoning to the unfathomable Mystery which it tries, forever vainly, to comprehend.
—Aldous Huxley[1]

Nowhere does our individuality show itself so cunningly and clearly as in the "varieties of religious experience." The religious experience of one person will never quite match that of another, nor, for that matter, will two visionary ecstasies of the same person ever be exactly the same. Scholars and religious institutions work hard to codify, regularize and generalize these experiences, but there is always something "left over" from these neatly described and categorized experiences which makes them unique. This uniqueness gives them their personal significance. This is why, to the man of such experience, William Blake, for example, the words of dogma and the levels of ecclesiastical preference seem so pale. For these reasons, the reader must expect no one-to-one relationship between the cases triggered by drugs, described in this chapter, compared with those noted in the last. He must use his intuition as well as his reason in comparing the two types. If he wishes to be more thorough, he will extend the knowledge of cases afforded in this volume by referring to the pages of Metzner, and Masters and Houston cited in Chapter 1. Best of all he will seek opportunities to observe psychedelic sessions at firsthand, following these up by talking to an unselected sampling of these cases, and hopefully, finding an appropriate opportunity to try the experience himself.

The Transcendental Atheist. Mr. D., a free-lance writer recently graduated from Harvard and estranged from the Jewish faith in which he was brought up, was one of a heroic group who volunteered to take LSD every day for sixteen days as part of a scientific investigation. His daily dosage was nearly 200 micrograms. At first, he greatly resented me as one of the supervisors, since I taught in a theological school and was interested in the religious parameters of the experiment. At the time, he rejected all religion and was a militant atheist. On the daily questionnaire he consistently described his sense of the presence of God as nil. Nevertheless, on other aspects of the experience associated with religion, such as a sense of rebirth, which he rated as "beyond anything ever experienced or imagined" previously, he presented a nature rich in those raw materials out of which profound religious experience is fashioned.

For the first few sessions he concentrated on personal conflicts and resentments, particularly toward his family. They culminated in a symbolic coming to terms with his father accompanied by highly dramatic, almost psychotic hostility, panic and terror. The experience ended with a symbolic resolution. Then, after acting out his own funeral, he seemed to reach a much quieter but inwardly creative phase. At this point he pointed out to me, for one thing, how much less crabbed and angular his handwriting had become. He still refused to interpret any of this development religiously.

On the next to the last day he was sitting on the grass idly watching the behavior of two grasshoppers. Suddenly they seemed to him to go into a kind of cosmic dance. This perception triggered a transcendental experience of great intensity and depth. At this point he spontaneously exclaimed that he had "seen God."

Nearly a year later I reviewed with him his experiences and their aftermath. He sees the whole as a religious experience, though in a highly transcendental, ineffable sense not closely related to institutional religion or a dogmatic, creedal theology. He was amazed to find that the growth he experienced was merely a beginning, and he feels that he has continued to mature ever since. When asked what he had learned through the sessions, he listed a sense of honesty in a variety of ways; a sense of "the enormously emotional fluid being beyond the ego, which had developed apart from certain basic elements; the sense of ways in which my total person had been fragmented and needed integrating"; and the acceptance of self and everything else in life, which was the key lesson.

A key experience was the death scene, which recurred spontaneously several times about five months later. He took care of the anxiety and confusion that these caused with another dose of LSD, when he deliberately restructured the scene with music. This resolved its problems. "The music wove me into a cocoon, and I burst out as a butterfly. This banished for me the meaning of death and led me into a dynamic acceptance of life and freedom from the fear of fear. This I had learned during the experiment, but it now was articulated. The experiences in the experiment became criteria toward which I could work, like the appreciation of music."

He spoke of his writing as now "more honest, less imitative, more authentic and creative." His humility had increased, along with his tolerance of others and ability to empathize with those whom he formerly was unable to endure—even "do-gooders." He now found himself more sensitive to pain and suffering and more "vulnerable," yet this became a stimulus to growth. "Life, both in its joys and pain has become more poignant—its problems more basic, simple and ultimate."

He also said that the subjects he chose for writing had changed markedly. He had moved away from the peripheral areas of life, where he thought he was an expert, into more competitive and more significant areas of interest. For example, he became deeply interested in the history of Plymouth Plantation, and he found that his experiences led him to identify with the Puritans. He now understood their motives in wishing to leave England where religion was prescribed for them and the reasons for their decline when they came into positions of authority. A year before, the subject would have bored him. A final interesting footnote is that his experiences with the grasshoppers made it impossible for him to kill even noxious insects for nearly a year after the experiment.

The Vision of Christ and a Passage to Joy. This describes the session of the Miss H., ordained minister in a Midwest Protestant parish, who was given a psychedelic drug by a psychotherapist. As might be expected, much of the resulting ecstasy produced Christian symbolism in highly immediate and vivid images which included an experience of the crucifixion similar to that of the armed robber with whose case we started this volume.

After a very pleasant optical phase, the next phase was psychotomimetic, a world filled with moving, threatening, steel machines. Contact with the real world seemed gone, but when the state was acknowledged as psychotic, fear diminished. From here the subject moved into a world of vast, radiant, indescribable light suggesting the presence of friendly power and flames through which she could have walked unharmed. At this point there came a sense of being in God and God being One, of which she was a part. This, she declared later, was in some ways similar to a mystical experience she had had earlier in her life, though different in other ways. The former had suddenly turned her life in a religious direction, which this experience confirmed. She remembered the drug experience much more clearly.

At this point she seemed to share "God's view of humanity" destroying itself in petty wars, which she was powerless to stop. She seemed to love these people, even in their weaknesses. She experienced a "magnificent vision of Christ," and though he was intangible, she could grasp his feet and ankles "with an infinite love." Then as the scene partly shifted back to God, like Saint Teresa, she seemed to understand the Trinity; and like Christ, she "took on all the pain of the world," and so experienced, in immediate form, the purpose of the crucifixion. Then came an acute sense of killing Christ through her ambition, lust, desire and pride. A storm symbolized the crucifixion, and she felt loved in her shame and disgrace. These three phases seemed to be the crux of her experience—"the oneness in God, the vision of Christ, the crucifixion."

From here she went on to a kind of "dying into the oneness of God" and a being born once again into humanity. "I dreaded the moment of birth. But I knew I must." Somehow she seemed to feel that the experience was to help her control her desires and solve her problems. This marked the beginning of the phase of "reentry." She became paranoid as she relived traumatic sexual experiences of her youth and sensed herself a confused adulteress. The real world seemed like "a puppet show, a dream, a masquerade, a game." She became filled with gratitude toward her psychotherapist, who was guiding her, and "asked God to love him." Finally, she felt sudden release from tension and a feeling of blessedness and peace. Her session ended with an overwhelming flood of joy.[2]

Since Miss H. is the "modern mystic" described in the last chapter, the reader can compare the two experiences. She stated that her first experience, which ushered her into the religious life, was far more influential, but that it was similar to the second one. But the latter enhanced remarkably her ability to empathize with the mentally ill encountered in her ministry.

In the symbolism of the ecstasy, one can sense the appearance of the problems of the subject as well as possible solutions to the problems. For example, the early psychotic phase probably reflected her fear of insanity, while the recognition of this fear immediately lessened it. The presence of the familiar therapist aided a proper resolution of this fear and paved the way to the religious phase of the experience on which Miss H. seems to set the most value. This stage may be compared to her mystical experience without benefiit of drugs described in the previous chapter. Without the presence of her sympathetic and supporting guide, Miss H. might well have gotten "hung up" on one of the psychotic phases and been deprived of the rewarding experience of joy with which the account ended.

The Ordeal of a Psychotherapist.[3] Authorities well acquainted with the psychedelic experience and those who are not express concern with what is termed "the bad trip." Those not well acquainted with it, however, are much more likely to become alarmed at its dangers. The dangers are there, and in the previous chapters I have pointed out the intuitive sensing of them by biblical personalities in their experiences of the *mysterium tremendum.* However, the average psychotherapist underestimates the value of facing frightening aspects of oneself. Even though these confrontations of self may involve temporary psychosis, they can be enormously maturing and strengthening if they are properly handled. The key, as Plato seems to have realized, is courage. It is the courage to face unwelcome revelations of ourselves, which may turn weaknesses into strength. The following account of a "bad trip" illustrates this truth.

Dr. H. is a well-known and respected psychotherapist, writer and a Quaker. Following a mystical experience on 50 mg. of psilocybin, he tried 300 seeds of morning glory eight months later. In his first experience, he felt that he had not completely "let go" in order to merge completely with the "Cosmic Mind," and he hoped in this experience to do so. While the experiment was pretty much on his own, he was fortunate to have his wife nearby for support in times of stress and need. This value was ambivalent, since his dependency interfered with that complete surrender of self which he deemed so important.

The stringency of the ordeal came from the terror of facing the inexorable logic of two loyalties. The one was to answer the call of the Ultimate, a bottomless abyss leading to complete loss of his individual self, resulting in a terrifying commitment to the life of the spirit, a willingness to leave behind position, goods, security and family, if necessary, to heed the call of the living God. To "lose his life in order to find it" was not a pious biblical phrase; it was an awesome leap in the dark. Biblical phrases besieged his mind: Isaiah's "I am a man of unclean lips," and God's word to Moses, "No man can look on God and live." Later on he wrote, "Your silence arises from having seen that to talk to God implies a discipleship which you cannot fulfill. You really want to die in bed at seventy-five." Then he realized that to benefit from this experience would mean a self-immolation he was not willing to face. The crucified Christ came to his mind, and he realized that he was not ready to lose his life to find it. He suddenly comprehended the meaning of the words and deeds of biblical personalities to whom all his life he had given lip loyalty. The realization shook him to his foundations!

Along with the struggle with these spiritual imperatives, fear of a more secular nature developed. In his terrified apprehension of the meaning of surrender he knew how fearful a thing it is to "fall into the hands of the living God!" If he acknowledged his panic and sought help, he might well be put into a mental hospital and lose his job. As a psychotherapist and one whose professional self was "sold to psychiatry," there could hardly be a disgrace worse than to be identified with the mentally ill, those helpless unfortunates whose misery had led him to dedicate his life to saving others. He would be a physician who could not heal himself. Like Job, the finger of scorn would be pointed at him, and he would be certified by society as a failure according to his own preachings. The wisdom of the world contended against the wisdom of the spirit. Values fought values, but fascination and integrity kept him enthralled in this awesome battle. Retreat would have been cowardice. And so continued what he called "the great straddling," between "the consolations of a psychiatric view and the demands of a religious one." He was learning "how shattering it was to move experientially from a personal, psychologically-oriented frame of reference into a wider, spiritual one." Afterward, he reflected that he had been asking the wrong questions and facing the wrong dichotomy. Either alternative, even the mental hospital, would have been tolerable, if he had been able to yield to it. In other words, he concluded that true spiritual progress is possible only through surrender.

In summary, he sees in his experience elements of psychotic delusion and a glimpse of reality. He discovered that for some, the depths of reality can be opened only by a dangerous flirting with the shadows of insanity. A. T. Boisen, William James and others whose moments of religious ecstasy we have briefly reviewed would have agreed with him.

These cases will also help to clarify the reasons why so many psychiatrists sound dark warnings about psychedelic drugs, and why there is nothing that the more traditional churches fear so much as ecstatic religious experience. Yet every single one of those whose ecstasies have been described, whether drug-induced or not, would reply as unhesitatingly as Miss H. did when she was asked if she wished to be free of the consequences of her moments of ecstasy. She said, "I would rather be dead than be the person I was before the vision!"

Dr. H. expressed this opinion of his "bad trip" and his moments of excruciating spiritual anguish: "Bad trips may ultimately be good ones. The way up is the way down. Spiritual gains are never made without risk . . . The great doubt, the abyss, the terror of reality are facts of inner experience whose validity and import-ance the present age must acknowledge."

Lucifer and the War with God. The final case in this chapter is the most detailed and dramatic in a book, *The Varieties of Psychedelic Experience,* by Masters and Houston,[4] which al-ready been mentioned. This case illustrates the remarkable agency of the drug to effect, in some persons, wholesome and profound personality change.

The person involved is referred to only as the subject. He is described as a very successful psychotherapist and college teacher in his late thirties, the only child of Protestant Anglo-Saxon parents with whom his relations are good. Wizened and ill al-most from birth, he surprised the doctors by surviving and de-veloping into a healthy manhood. Precociously intelligent, he early thought of himself as different and "alien to the human race." At the same time, he found himself irresistibly attracted toward "what others regarded as evil"; though, like criminal psychopaths, who have described to me their predrug conscious-ness, his own conscience was never troubled. He enjoyed the manipulation of others for its own sake, sexual promiscuity and the encouragement of "evil" in others. He identified with the devil rather than with God, though he was always shrewd enough to keep out of serious trouble. He was, at the same time, a very able psychotherapist and was regarded by many as a kind, compassionate person.

In his twenties he developed serious neurotic symptoms. For a time it was practically impossible for him "to *ask* anybody for anything" without severe agitation. He attacked these symptoms in a seven-year course of self-analysis, including autohypnosis, with the result that he brought the symptoms under control. At the same time, he began to feel his interest in the devil juvenile and began to strive toward "that genuine source of strength and inner peace men call God." Though he felt he had made much progress, he was not completely satisfied. This led him, a year or so later, to volunteer as a subject in an experiment with LSD.

In the first session, the subject seemed to witness the creation, with an evolutionary force tending to perfect God's work in conflict with another force tending to destroy it. He described himself as ambivalent, "wanting to side with God, but somehow allied with the other force that incessantly strives to turn order into chaos." In these symbols he sensed a clue to his own nature.

In his second session, a week later, the subject seemed to witness a tremendous battle between gigantic beasts, which he identified as forces within himself which would be threatened with extinction should he abandon himself to God. He questioned whether he should "dare to meet him unless properly prepared." The battle evolved into one where he seemed to alternate between surrender to God and defiance him. At about this point he saw for the first time that his life was a "recapitulation of Lucifer's struggle with God." His central problem had been pride. He considered the second session extremely productive—much more so than more conventional psychotherapeutic techniques, such as psychoanalysis.

His third and last session occurred the following week. Very fearfully he awaited a "meeting with God." His symbolization continued to be highly dramatic and complex. Among the important happenings a few may be singled out. He perceived the figurine of a mermaid that was handed to him as the personification of evil, until he realized that he was projecting evil onto the figurine. Therefore, it was he who was making of God's gift evil or good. He also realized that, though there were other ways of explaining his life, and though he regretted not being able to put his understandings into scientific-medical language, somehow the mythical terminology best suited his case, such as, the revolt of Lucifer, God and devil, heaven and hell. "I would prefer not to have these naked truths stated so bluntly, but rather frosted over with lots of high-sounding medical terminology."

Shortly after this he saw himself gaining strength, not to master others but rather to master himself. "With the knowledge I have I can then use my strength to help others."

The guide now suggested that the time had come for him to drop his resistance and face God. Amid symbolism as vivid as the vision of a Hebrew prophet and with much emotion, he "experienced the Presence of God," in which he allowed himself to "weep tears of gladness," and symbolically "shook himself free" from those roots that had been binding him to hell.

It is always difficult to assess any change in personality, particularly when the process is so profoundly subjective as it was in this case. It can also be seriously misleading to assume that change has taken place with no objective check on the results. One year later, the subject felt that he could offer objective evidence to support his own conviction of fundamental change. He noted that the number of patients he could handle and his literary output had increased. He also felt the quality of his work to be higher. He had become more gregarious and enjoyed participating in social activities in which previously he had no interest. He had fallen in love and was planning to be married to a woman his equal. He was no longer promiscuous, nor did he seek the society of those so inferior he could dominate them. In general, he felt that "a destructive response to the world had been replaced by an essentially creative response."

One aim of the last two chapters is to suggest the power of inner religious experience to mediate wholesome personality change, whether that experience has been initiated by a drug or not. Another has been to suggest at least a family resemblance between the drug-induced and non-drug-induced experience. In later chapters I will present more scientific evidence in support of this resemblance. This will lead to one of the questions posed by the book: Is it possible and wise for men to use the psychedelic materials to initiate religious experience—not only to study the religious consciousness but, more importantly, to transform people and so to help them?

Going beyond the issue of whether or not religious experience may be drug-induced, these chapters—and the book as a whole —aim to give the reader a feeling for ecstatic religious experience, to help him to distinguish it from that pale affair which the average churchgoer encounters in his weekly visit to his place of worship. It will help him to understand the sources of real power in personal religion, and to discover the reason why there are so many who neither fear nor respect the average religious institution. It will also give him a glimpse of what impelled the writer of Hebrews to exclaim, "It is a fearful thing to fall into the hands of the living God!" He may begin to understand the writer's blissful ecstasy at the contemplation of the infinitude of God's creation, "When the morning stars sang together, and all the sons of God shouted for joy!"

NOTES

1. Aldous Huxley, *The Doors of Perception* (New York: Harper, 1954), p. 79.
2. Abstracted from R. Metzner, *The Ecstatic Adventure* (New York: Macmillan, 1968), chap. 7. The case is one of many drug-induced ecstasies to be found in the book.
3. Abstracted from *Ibid.*, chap. 4.
4. R. E. L. Masters and J. Houston, *Varieties of Psychedelic Experience,* last chapter.

4. Historical Notes:
The Harvard Incident

Now, tell me, has any god bestowed on mankind a specific to induce fear—a drug whose effect is that the more a man permits himself to imbibe of it, the darker he fancies his fortune at every draught, present and future alike grow increasingly alarming, and the climax is abject terror in the bravest, though when the subject has recovered from his stupor and shaken off the effects of the potion, he regularly becomes his own man again? . . . a touchstone of the courage or cowardice of your citizens?
—Plato[1]

Cambridge, Massachusetts, U.S.A., was no place to start a new religion. —Timothy Leary[2]

But it matters not if some or even most prophets have been vain or false, if there are any true prophets. In this, as in other great matters, nature makes a thousand failures to bring forth one consummate product. The existence of the genuine mystic— Bernard, Mohammed, Lao Tze, Plotinus, Eckhart, John of the Cross—however seldom he is found, is the momentous thing; sufficient to command respect for the tradition of mysticism, sufficient to justify the attention which through religious history has been focussed upon these individuals.
—William Ernest Hocking[3]

Religious experience under the influence of almost any drug, including alcohol, cannot be completely ruled out, but we are discussing specifically the so-called "hallucinogenic" or "psychedelic" drugs. The latter term, literally "mind manifesting," is

40

used when one has the ecstatic or visionary properties of the drugs in mind, hence its use in this volume. They include the LSD-type drugs, chiefly psilocybin and mescaline, in addition to LSD. New psychedelic chemicals, like DMT, DPT, STP, and other psychedelics similar in their effects to LSD, are still being synthesized, and similar properties are being discovered in many plants and herbs. My own research has convinced me that marihuana must be considered a mild psychedelic and, therefore, can trigger religious experience. The present chapter is designed to put the religious use of the drugs in historical perspective and to bring the story up-to-date.

Religious Uses of Drugs Among the Ancients. There is no doubt that chemicals played a part in many ancient religions, though just what part is hard to assess with any precision. The cannabis, or hemp plant, from which marihuana is derived, was described in Chinese literature in 2737 B.C., and introduced into India before 800 B.C.[4] That marihuana may have had some early religious significance is suggested by the discovery of a funerary urn in Wilmersdorf, Germany, which dated back to the fifth century, B.C. It contained particles of the seeds of the hemp plant. A religious use of hemp has also been discovered among the natives in the Belgian Congo.[5] Marihuana in the form known as *bhang* is used in India in certain Hindu rites,[6] though, like other aspects of these drugs, the origins of this use are lost in history.

Even though we cannot trace its exact features, there is pretty clear evidence of the religious use of psychedelic drugs among the ancient Greeks. The priestesses at Delphi inhaled certain vapors issuing from the earth, which brought on ecstatic conditions during which their famous prophecies were spoken. Even more significant were the Eleusinian Mysteries. Initiates to this cult underwent an ordeal involving, among other things, drinking a potion that dramatically altered the state of the initiate's consciousness and led to knowledge not granted ordinary mortals. Since the initiate was sworn to secrecy by a solemn oath, and no account of the breaking of this oath exists, we can only guess at the nature of the potion. Plato was supposed to have been an initiate, and a passage in *The Laws* refers to a hypothetical drug of a frightening nature proposed as a "touchstone of courage," a virtue highly valued by Plato as one of the characteristics of the responsible citizen and ruler. Those who have experienced the modern psychedelics seem convinced that Plato was making veiled reference to his own ordeal.[7] That he had had some kind of profound ecstatic experience very influential in his thinking is indicated by the famous Parable of the Cave, found in the Seventh Book of *The Republic*. Ingesters of LSD have had no trouble in recognizing and understanding the metaphysical dimensions of this notable piece of classical symbolism.

There are also historical indications of the use of cannabis drugs in the Moslem faith, though not among the traditional Moslem mystics, or Sufis, where we might expect it. Hashish, a concentrated form of marihuana, was used religiously by the "Hashishins," the original name of the Isma'ili branch of the Shiite sect, which flourished in the Near East from the eleventh century until its political suppression in the thirteenth. To this sect we owe the modern word *assassin*, stemming from the custom of the leaders of the sect to delegate to fanatical followers the task of killing political enemies.

The religious use of hashish by this sect was secret, and surrounded in considerable mystery. Contemporaries believed that hashish fanned the "assassins" into a fury of killing. Similar fancies are current today relative to the psychedelics. However, anyone familiar with the qualities of hashish would be inclined to doubt the murderous effects of the drug. It would probably have precisely the opposite effect—the user would be friendly rather than hostile. The motive for the assassinations undoubtedly came from the political ambitions and strategies of successive Hashishin leaders.[8] Hashish was more likely used as a kind of spiritual reward.

In a volume just published, R. Gordon Wasson has pretty well established the *Amanita Muscaria* mushroom as the source of the fabled *soma* of ancient India, according to the ethnobotanist R. E. Schultes of Harvard. It satisfies descriptive details and evidence gathered from Vedic hymns, while no contradictory evidence has been found. Soma was worshipped and deified in the *Rig Veda*.[8A]

More contemporary, but beginning in prehistory, is the use of various hallucinogenic plants and fungi by the Aztecs and various American-Indian peoples, in both North and South America. The early Spanish explorers in the sixteenth century reported, with disgust and a sense of Christian outrage, "orgies" attending religious rites when the sacred mushroom, or "God's flesh," along with morning glory and other herbs, was consumed.

Obscure descendants of these once proud religious devotees still continue their rites in the South American wilds. In the dark of night during the rainy season when mushrooms abound in the back country Mexican mountain hamlets, priests and priestesses still officiate in ceremonies featuring their sacramental consumption. Most visible today, however, is the Native American Church, said to number perhaps a quarter of a million adherents spread throughout most of the prominent Indian tribes.[9] This is a federation of North American Indian users of peyote, prepared from the bud, or mescal button of the cactus plant. (From peyote scientists isolated its chief active principle, mescaline, on the basis of pioneer investigation of peyote reported by Havelock Ellis and S. Weir Mitchel before the turn of the century.)[10]

For many years these Indians have been harassed by Indian agents and jealous missionaries, who find them very difficult to convert. They have also been opposed by nonmembers among their own people. Most of the arguments against LSD—that it drives people insane and debases their morals—have parallels in Indian controversies over peyote. Although many of these Indians have suffered imprisonment rather than give up their religious use of peyote, whenever laws governing its religious use have been tested in the courts, they usually have been over-turned, because no hard evidence has been found that peyote, in this context, does harm. Indeed, there is much evidence that it does good. The Native American Church claims that it is Christian, and its moral teachings of family responsibility, hard work, love of one another and abstinence from alcohol does not depart markedly from the teachings of the typical American middle class Christian churches. Anthropologists generally have spoken with approval of the dignity of its services, when peyote is consumed in night-long ceremonies, and of the superior effectiveness of lives of the members.[11]

The Modern Phase of the Use of the Psychedelics. The modern phase of the investigation and use of the psychedelics began in 1938, when the brilliant Swiss biochemist, Albert Hofmann, discovered and synthesized what he christened "d-lysergic acid diethylamide tartrate-25" (LSD for short) as the result of research with the products of fermented rye. Several years later he discovered its psychoactive properties by accidentally ingesting a tiny portion of the drug, perhaps not more than 50 millionths of a gram, which gives an indication of its potency. From the beginning, Hofmann was aware of the religious potentialities of LSD. Most scientists and physicians, not much interested in religion, saw in it chiefly a means of producing temporary madness and began to call this class of drugs "psychotomimetic."

At the same time some psychotherapists began to see it, not so much as a means of creating mental illness, as of treating it. With this purpose in mind, the late Max Rinkel, M.D., introduced it in the United States and encouraged its scientific study.

During the fifties, Canadian scientists became interested. The best known among them were Abram Hoffer and Humphry Osmond. The latter coined the term "psychedelic" in response to his observation that subjects often discovered sensitivities and capacities within themselves that they never would have suspected had it not been for the influence of the drugs. Hoffer and Osmond did important pioneer work on the use of LSD in the rehabilitation of alcoholics, and discovered, to their surprise, that the key to its effectiveness seemed to reside in its religious properties. I will describe this work in a later chapter.

Another fascinating chapter in psychedelic discovery was written through the hobby of a New York banker and his wife, Gordon and Valentina Wasson, amateur mycologists. Their interest in mushrooms led them from one species to another until they encountered the sacred mushrooms of Mexico. In June, 1955, they journeyed to the Sierra Mazateca in Oaxaca, and were probably the first outsiders to eat the mushroom as part of the mushroom rite. Their religious experiences and subsequent insights into, and interest in, the religious significance of the mushrooms have been discussed under several scholarly titles.[12] This interest led to collaboration with the French mycologist, Roger Heim, and the subsequent synthesis of the active principle of the mushrooms, psilocybin, the drug with which Dr. Timothy Leary later began his researches.

In the fifties, Aldous Huxley, who had an interest in the mystical consciousness and had written several volumes touching on it, also tried this direct method of studying it. In May, 1953, he "turned on" with four-tenths of a gram of mescaline. His publication in 1954 of an account of his experiences in *The Doors of Perception* constituted something of a literary event.[13] For the first time, large numbers of the educated public became aware of the phenomenology of one of the psychedelic drugs and of their relationship to religious experience. Having become convinced that the visionary and mystical forms of religion alone had power to change and shape personality at a deep level, Huxley advocated the use of mescaline as a safe and nonaddictive way to effective religious life. In this connection, he cited J. S. Slotkin's research about the peyote cult. Along with the theologian-scientist, Gerald Heard, and the writer, Alan Watts, he became associated with a group which has largely turned away from western forms of religion in favor of the eastern faiths with their greater emphasis on mysticism and the nonrational aspects of the religious life.

The Harvard Incident. Perhaps the most highly publicized, single happening in the history of the psychedelic drug movement was the summary dismissal of Dr. Timothy Leary from his post as lecturer at Harvard University. Its repercussions are not likely to be stilled during the present generation. Behind the scenes burned a whole complex of charges and countercharges, passionate loyalties and vicious meanness, painfully arrived at administrative decisions, ambitions thwarted and fulfilled, passions, rumors, jealousies, gossip, wisdom, and folly. It will be impossible to do complete justice to the intricacies of this witches' brew. I will confine myself to the barest outline of the facts as I knew them and carefully checked them, together with such interpretations as seem compatible with a responsible, but necessarily subjective, judgment of such controversial matters.[14]

From February, 1960, Dr. Leary held a position as lecturer in psychology in Harvard's Department of Social Relations. During the summer of 1960, with other scholars and friends, he tested the effect of the sacred mushroom of Mexico on himself. Almost immediately he saw the revolutionary possibilities of its active principle, psilocybin, and later LSD, for psychotherapy and religion.

After coming to Harvard, he continued to experiment with growing interest, involving some Harvard students as subject volunteers. Gradually, modestly funded research projects were developed, including the very promising pilot project for the rehabilitation of convicts at the Concord Prison, to be described later. Soon the use of student subjects aroused criticism and apprehension among Dr. Leary's colleagues and the Harvard administration. It was indicated to him that parents were objecting, and the effect of his research on public relations was pointed out more than once. Consequently, he and his faculty associate in the work, Richard Alpert, agreed to confine experimentation to graduate students only. Finally, Dr. Leary consented to entrust his supply of the drugs to Dr. Dana Farnsworth, Director of Harvard Health Services, with the understanding, at least on Dr. Leary's part, that they would be readily available for appropriate research.

Shortly after, when Dr. Walter Pahnke, with Leary's approval, desired access to these chemicals for the Good Friday Experiment, they were unavailable. Since the experiment had been sanctioned by Dr. Pahnke's faculty-appointed Harvard doctoral committee, Dr. Leary felt that Dr. Farnsworth had broken faith with him, if he had not deliberately tricked him. Dr. Farnsworth had been made aware of serious problems among some students using the drugs, and from these cases he had inferred high danger from psychedelic substances. He was in no way equipped as an expert in the sense that he had tried them on himself, observed any sessions from beginning to end or systematically followed up a randomly selected population of those who had been given the drugs. But he felt that to release the drugs for human experimentation would be irresponsible. Furthermore, guidelines for the use of the drug had not yet been worked out among all interested parties at Harvard, according to Dr. Farnsworth. The historic Good Friday Experiment was saved from being cancelled at the last minute only because Leary had previously given a supply of psilocybin to a researcher in a nearby city, who made enough available for the experiment.

The esteem of colleagues for Dr. Leary's work is indicated, not only by his being called to Harvard in the first place, but by offers of recommendation for tenure by two of his superiors, if he would only "lay off drugs" for a year or two. But by this time the Timothy Leary, brought to Harvard as a social scientist, was beginning to turn into a mystic and a poet with a prophetic sense of mission to change others as he had been changed through profound religious experience. As he has said, Harvard was no place to carry on research on visionary experience.[15] The process of mutual disenchantment had begun, and he whose adventurous course

> . . . with no middle flight intends to soar
> Above the Aonian mount, while it pursues
> Things unattempted yet . . .[16]

began to conceptualize the bold project of bringing what he now saw as an almost Promethean gift to a world, which seemingly has lost its way in materialism, greed and strife. His destiny became clearer to him with every hour. The Harvard "establishment" seemed to see only stubbornness and fanaticism. A drama of failure to communicate, so tragically constant in the history of conscientious men in authority with points of view different from the mystic and the prophet, was about to be played once again. One can only speculate what mistakes, on both sides, could have been avoided through mutual understanding. But this perception would have required of those making the administrative decisions some empathic discernment of the profound religious experience that had taken Timothy Leary captive. There was little evidence that they possessed this type of wisdom. Furthermore, for reasons that are at least partially clear, they were unwilling to take the risks involved in acquiring such wisdom by trying the drugs themselves.

The axe fell just a few weeks before Leary's contract was to expire. Toward the end of the academic year 1961-62, Dr. Leary had been informed that, despite his contract, he was to teach only part-time and was to be paid accordingly. He was listed in the catalog as teaching only in the spring semester of 1962-63. He asked his immediate superior, Professor David McClelland, permission to do all his teaching in the fall semester so that he could go to Mexico in March or April to set up a project for the International Federation for Internal Freedom. This request was granted, according to Dr. Leary. Professor McClelland, however, denies any recollection of the agreement. That there was nothing in writing was quite characteristic of Dr. Leary's habitual ways of dealing with people. Dr. McClelland asserts that his first awareness of Leary's absence came when a reporter in Los Angeles phoned to check on the authenticity of a report by Dr. Leary that he had been fired. McClelland states that this antedated the action of the Harvard Corporation on April 30, and that Leary could have avoided dismissal even then by returning to Cambridge.

When the spring semester of 1962-63 had begun, Dr. Leary assumed that his duties had been discharged. However, he consented to supervise the field work of two students at Bridgewater State Hospital. The students were informed that he intended leaving Cambridge in March. Actually, it was about the middle of April before he left. The fact of his absence was brought to the attention of the Harvard administration, and on May 6, 1963, the Harvard Corporation passed the following vote:

Voted: Because Timothy F. Leary, Lecturer on Clinical Psychology, has failed to keep his classroom appointments and has absented himself from Cambridge during term time without permisison, to relieve him from further teaching duty and to terminate his salary as of April 30, 1963.

The Corporation viewed his action as a clear violation of faculty rules and, therefore, not subject to a hearing,[17] although their decision was clearly contrary to principles governing Academic Tenure, Section 4, drawn up by representatives of the American Association of University Professors, and of the Association of American Colleges in 1940, and subscribed to officially by both Associations in 1941. Section 4 reads in part:

> . . . dismissal for cause of a teacher previous to the expiration of a term appointment, should, if possible, be considered by both a faculty committee and the governing board of the institution. In all cases where the facts are in dispute, the accused teacher should be informed before the hearing in writing of the charges against him and should have the opportunity to be heard in his own defense by all bodies that pass judgment upon his case.

These principles were reprinted in the summer, 1963, issue of the AAUP *Bulletin,* shortly after Dr. Leary's dismissal.

Whether Dr. Leary could have obtained a hearing, had he requested it at the time, will never be known, since he did not do so. He felt that even previous to this action he had been treated in an unfair and arbitrary manner. He had made up his mind that the work so important to him could not be done at Harvard, and had expected no extension of his contract beyond June 30, 1963. To have engaged in an altercation with Harvard over a few months' salary seemed to him a waste of his energies and a possible disservice to friends who were working with him.

There were some who felt that Harvard's action was a body blow to the principles of academic freedom. If Harvard, with its reputation as a defender of these principles and a bellwether of the academic flock, could dismiss a teacher *for any cause* without a hearing, then any institution could do the same. These people felt that the Harvard chapter of the AAUP should have called for an investigation of the case in the interest of academic freedom in general, whether Dr. Leary wished it or not.

But whatever the rights and wrongs of Harvard's or Dr. Leary's actions, there were certain clear, practical consequences bearing on the investigation and use of the psychedelic drugs. Whatever the technical reasons for the dismissal of Dr. Leary, and of his colleague, Dr. Richard Alpert, about the same time but on different grounds, the public and most of the Harvard community considered the controversy over the use of the drugs to be the basic factor. Though there were many on the faculty and elsewhere who accepted Dr. Farnsworth's judgment of the danger of the drugs, there were others who differed, and who believed that investigation of their effects on human beings should go forward. The dismissal effectively frightened many who might have pursued controlled study of the drugs at Harvard and elsewhere. Few wished to risk loss of reputation or position. Many of Leary's former friends dropped him. The Massachusetts Mental Health Center, partly under Harvard's direction, afterward pursued some carefully controlled research with psilocybin under the direction of Dr. Walter N. Pahnke and others. However, even this was soon stopped by order of the trustees.

The damage done to the principles of academic freedom cannot be calculated, but there is no doubt that they were considerable. I am reporting just a few cases of pressure that I happen to know about. A professor of psychology, known to be interested in the drugs, was summoned before the president of his institution's board of trustees (not Harvard) and threatened with summary dismissal unless he promised to stop all experimentation and never to mention the drugs again in his classes. A Harvard student who had been associated with Dr. Leary in his research with convicts, narrowly escaped dismissal from his field work position by the respected director of a Boston mental health agency. Another graduate associate, who had received high recommendations from his Harvard professors for a teaching appointment elsewhere, was immediately dropped from consideration when his research with psychedelic drugs was discovered.

But Dr. Leary's rejection by the Harvard community had another more subtle result. He felt that they treated him in an unsympathetic, unjust and inhumane way. It seemed that Harvard had been afflicted with a failure of nerve. When the chips were down, institutional preservation prevailed over open-mindedness and the search for truth. The inhumanity of the method of his dismissal completed his disenchantment with the establishment in general, and the academic establishment in particular. This helps to explain his radical appeal to the youth of America, the only segment of society that seems to him sufficiently courageous to experiment on themselves with the psychedelics, and sufficiently free from prejudice to consider the truths with which the visionary experience confronted them. Hence his advice, "Don't trust anyone over thirty!" and "Turn on, Tune in and Drop out!"

If some with grey hair and a liking for their entrenched power of position and faith in the affluent and achieving society, deplore the ways of Leary's followers, they may well ask themselves whether the situation they deplore is not in large part a product of the failure in communication within the Harvard community, and the abrupt action of dismissal. I have heard it estimated by a public relations expert that the dismissal, with an able assist by the U. S. goverment, which subsequently arrested Leary, was worth several millions of dollars of free publicity. If Harvard's aims were to disseminate Dr. Leary's views as widely as possible among young and old, it could hardly have performed more superbly.

This is not a judgment between Dr. Leary and Harvard, nor a pretense that Harvard made all the mistakes, and that Dr. Leary made none. He can see mistakes he regrets, and he is not unsympathetic with the dilemma of those who forced his rejection. Furthermore, Harvard has made some amends by throwing fewer obstacles in the way of his subsequent lecturing on the campus than other less secure universities do. But there is no doubt that, if Harvard had weathered the storm for the few remaining weeks of his contract, fewer young people would now be engaging in rebellious and frivolous experimentation with the drugs. And the free academic marketplace with respect to ideas about these drugs would be less restricted. For one example, it is a shameful impoverishment of the debate on the drugs that so few institutions are willing to hear the views of Dr. Leary himself, who probably has had more varied experience with the psychedelics than anyone in the world, and whose intuitions about them are penetrating.

Since leaving Harvard, Dr. Leary's history has included a series of harassments of himself and his family. About a year later, he was arrested on the charge of "smuggling" when a small amount of marihuana was found on his daughter. Apparently, he was framed by collusion of Mexican and United States customs agents on the Texas border. His sentence of thirty years in federal prison and a $30,000 fine was reversed by the United States Supreme Court in May, 1969. About this time he incorporated the League for Spiritual Discovery as a religious institution with headquarters at Millbrook, N.Y. The League maintained its constitutional right to use drugs religiously. A posse of fifteen police agents raided the premises in the dead of night, wakened his guests and undressed the women in the search for evidence. Inconsequential amounts of marihuana, unknown to Leary, were found on a visiting couple. Leary was handcuffed and arrested. A few weeks later the charges were dropped. But more recently, at the instigation of the townspeople, he was again arrested; his son was abused by the police and he was forced to close down. Most recently, in the fall of 1968, he was arrested by the police in Laguna Beach, California for double-parking. The occupants of his car were searched, and marihuana was found on his son. Again he was arrested and now faces charges.

A Clue to the Personality of Dr. Leary. I cannot resist the desire to comment on this attractive enigma, Timothy Leary. A clue to his personality will also be a clue to many an "acid head" and, therefore, a step toward understanding the drug movement and its significance, which may be crucial to our society. The clue I have in mind is in William James' chapter on saintliness in his *Varieties.* James does not give the conventional picture of the saint but relies on his original intuitions. Had his spirit been invoked at Harvard during the Leary controversy, it would almost certainly have spoken on Leary's side.

James speaks of the saint having "a feeling of being in a wider life than that of this world's selfish little interests; and a conviction, not merely intellectual, but as it were sensible, of an Ideal Power."[18] To most of Leary's academic associates no goal can be imagined higher than achieving a full professorship at Harvard, with tenure and the emoluments, tangible and intangible, that go with such achievement—unless it be more of the same type of reward. To them, any person who would knowingly pass up such an opportunity must truly be mad. It was behavior of this type that won for the psychedelic drugs the reputation for warping the judgment of those who ingested them. Nevertheless, most of those who tried them did glimpse that wider world in which Timothy Leary lives.

James quotes Henry Drummond's phrase, "the expulsive power of a higher affection."[19] It is this headlong force of the "higher affection" that marks the saint and makes nonsense of all the lesser values of sober society. The ordinary Christian can tolerate church only because he can close his ears to the invitation to saintliness. He can ignore Jesus' call to leave father and mother, son and daughter, to cast aside his nets and business—in modern terms to "drop out"—and follow him. Similarly, Socrates was reproved by his neighbors for living a life of idleness, "corrupting the youth" of Athens. The citizens of Assisi closed their doors to the ragged band of "hippies" who scrounged food and practiced poverty with Francis. The sober, unimaginative, hardworking and conscientious citizen should not be despised any more than should the conscientious Harvard administrator or department head, who is responsible for the welfare of many students. Circumscribed by values that they understand, they perform the necessary chores of serving society. In doing so, they must also obey their inhibitions and say, "No, no!" instead of "shifting the emotional centre towards loving and harmonious affections, towards 'yes, yes' where the claims of the non-ego are concerned." In James' view, this is another mark of the saint.

Timothy Leary exhibits this absolute commitment also, for he is nothing if not a permissive and hospitable man, although he can be stubborn when one man imposes his standards on another. He calls this "tyranny." One senses "the friendly continuity of the ideal power" with his own life, the "surrender to its control" and the "immense elation and freedom" of which James speaks. Leary's equanimity, keenness of mind, his sense of humor, empathy and compassion under misfortunes, which would crush ordinary men, would be impossible were it not linked to some source of strength in that wider life James also connects with "strength of soul."[20]

This freedom from conventional values has opened the eyes of the despised and rejected to the virtues of saintliness more often than it has convinced respectable men. Jesus was depreciated for mingling with publicans and sinners, and the outcasts and lepers followed Francis long before his respectable neighbors in Assisi listened to him. So with Leary. He knowingly welcomed ex-convicts to his house. Two of them, to the alarm of the neighbors, lived with him. An armed robber told me that Dr. Leary was the first man he had ever met who was, he felt, unequivocally on his side. Another robber said that, in his thirty-odd years of a life of crime, Leary was the only man he had ever known about whom convicts never had a critical word. Of course, it could be claimed that both of these men were prejudiced, for in an experiment on the use of psilocybin, Dr. Leary had psychologically and spiritually raised them from the dead!

All this is not to say that Timothy Leary is a second Jesus Christ, Socrates, or Francis of Assisi. He is only a first Timothy Leary. He is a human being who has made his share of mistakes. He is a complex man to whom I have offered merely one clue. For a definitive picture, we must wait a long time.

In terms of the "wider life," of which James has spoken, the perspective of time is required to bring out true spiritual greatness or the lack of it. Time will tell whether Timothy Leary is a pied piper or one of the perceptive prophets of the age. His aims, his personality and the sources of his insights and energies dictate that he be judged by the criteria James describes in his discussion of saintliness.

William Ernest Hocking once spoke of the true mystic or authentic prophet as one man in a thousand. He agrees with James in seeing saintliness as the best thing that history has to show. But here, he says, nature makes a thousand failures to one success.[21] I do not know whether Timothy Leary represents a failure or a success. But if I had to gamble on one or the other, I would wager on success!

The Development of Psychedelic Churches. If the type of religion uncovered by the psychedelic drugs is ever to influence the main stream of western religious life, it will probably have its rise, like most vigorous religious movements, outside the main line religious institutions. Historically this has nearly always been the case, for fresh movements seem radical to the average institutional observer. In addition, the nonrational energies which they release, if they are powerful enough to "redeem" human nature, may occasionally cause personal breakdowns and unsettling confusion. These considerations, combined with a multitude of vested interests, make the religious institutions a hard nut to crack. Consequently, it is not surprising that any experience so powerful and so esoteric as that released by the psychedelic drugs should be kept at arm's length by the orthodox churchmen who will scornfully refer to the "psychedelic churches" as "cults." I use the term "cult" in a descriptive, not judgmental, sense. In some ways the term is interchangeable with the word "church." The "psychedelic churches" *are* churches, at least in an embryonic sense.

I have already referred to the Native American Church, the most clearly defined and the most traditional of the psychedelic churches or cults. Its membership is restricted almost wholly to Indians. But there are a number of religious organizations that have been formed with the idea of making the psychedelic sacrament a central or very important element in worship. There is a tendency in many of these to form a community, a not untraditional aspect of the beginnings of many religious movements, such as the early Christians, monastic orders or Hasidic communities.[22]

One of the most visible of the psychedelic churches is the League for Spiritual Discovery formed by Dr. Leary. I have already spoken of its harassment by neighbors and the police, again a not untraditional experience for cultic groups. A second example is the Neo-American Church, founded by the Reverend Arthur Kleps, who calls himself Chief Boo Hoo of the Church.

Many people, including some judges, hardly know whether to take him as a religious leader or a professional funny man. However, in an appearance before the Special Senate Judiciary Subcommittee on Narcotics in Washington on May 25, 1966, Mr. Kleps left no doubt that he considered the religious use of the psychedelic drugs a right which the Constitution confers on any citizen, and which he and his followers intend to exercise.

There have been reports of an open Neo-American communion service in a Washington, D.C., park on Easter Sunday, April 6, 1969, with peyote the sacramental element. This attempt to test the constitutionality of the drug laws was frustrated by the refusal of the police to make any arrests. However, on the following day, Mr. Kleps invaded a public building where he could not be ignored and the arrest followed.

In justification of his somewhat jocular treatment of his own church, Mr. Kleps points out that through the ages the church institution has been the great enemy of the interior religious spirit. To refuse to take himself and his own church organization seriously is to build in a protection against institutionalization. To do him justice, it must be said that occasionally he has refused to depart from this principle even when his church seemed to have something temporal to gain by doing so. I do not necessarily approve of all the practices of the Neo-American Church. But I see no reason to doubt that Arthur Kleps is a religious man. At the very least, in company with Erasmus and Dean Swift, he is a keen ecclesiastical satirist.

A third organization within this growing movement is the more conservative Church of the Awakening, incorporated as a religious institution in Socorro, New Mexico, in 1963. The founders are two retired physicians, Doctors John and Louisa Aiken, who had often administered both peyote and mescaline sacramentally before the spate of punitive legislation against any use of the psychedelics. This group is a fellowship dedicated to the religious quest by any effective means, of which the psychedelic sacrament is not only important but essential. Membership does not preclude membership in other religious bodies. So far, the church has stayed within the law as a matter of policy and has applied, so far unsuccessfully, to the Bureau of Narcotics and Dangerous Drugs of the Justice Department for permission to use peyote for sacramental purposes. When all legal recourse has been exhausted, the church intends to resort to a test case.

Other similar institutions include Naturalism, Incorporated, headed by Mr. George Peters of Chicago, another psychedelic leader recently jailed. Naturalism maintains a free service for helping people on "bad trips" and guiding users to distinguish the addictive drugs, like heroin and alcohol, from the nonaddictive psychedelics. Still another body, according to reports, is the Church of the Clear Light on the West Coast. In addition to those bodies that are incorporated, there are any number of nonincorporated psychedelic bodies and communities of greatly varying quality and levels of responsibility.

With the passage of time there seems to be a tendency for these bodies to rely on psychedelic drugs less rather than more. The successful groups have seen the necessity for a discipline to govern household management and to set at least implicit standards of personal behavior. Nearly all members of such psychedelic communities use marihuana freely and have used the more potent drugs like LSD at least once. One very rarely finds anyone, whether a member or nonmember, or one who has given up the drugs, who is sorry that he took them in the first place.[23]

NOTES

1. Plato, "A Touchstone for Courage," *Psychedelic Review*, 1, No. 1 (Summer, 1963), pp. 43-46.
2. Timothy Leary, *High Priest* (Cleveland: World Publishing Co., 1968), p. 320.

3. William Ernest Hocking, *The Meaning of God in Human Experience* (New Haven: Yale University Press, 1912), p. 349.

4. See W. H. McGlothlin in D. Solomon, ed., *The Marihuana Papers* (New York: New American Library, 1966), p. 455.

5. W. Reininger in *Ibid.*, pp. 141-142.

6. See G. C. Carstairs in *Ibid, passim*, especially pp. 112-113, 119.

7. Plato, "A Touchstone for Courage," *Psychedelic Review*, 1, No. 1 (1963); R. Gordon Wasson, "The Hallucinogenic Fungi of Mexico," *Ibid.*, pp. 27-42.

8. *Encyclopedia Britannica*, 11th ed., s. v. "Assassin"; N. Taylor, "The Pleasant Assassin" in D. Solomon, ed., *The Marihuana Papers*, pp. 31-47. Also see titles by M. Hodgson on the Hashishins.

8A. R. G. Wasson, *Soma: Divine Mushroom of Immortality* (New York: Harcourt, Brace & World, 1969); R. E. Schultes, "Hallucinogens of Plant Origin" *Science*, 163 (January 17, 1969), pp. 245-254.

9. For an account of American hallucinogenic plants, with allusions to religion and history, see R. E. Schultes, "Botanical Sources of New World Narcotics," *Psychedelic Review*, 1, No. 2 (1963), pp. 145-166. With A. Hofmann, Dr. Schultes is now at work on a book, *The Botany and Chemistry of Hallucinogens* (Springfield, Ill.: Chas. C. Thomas, probably 1970).

10. See R. S. de Ropp, *Drugs and the Mind* (New York: Grove Press, 1960), chapter on mescaline.

11. See D. Aberle, *The Peyote Religion Among the Navaho* (Chicago: Aldine, 1966); J. S. Slotkin, *The Peyote Religion* (Glencoe, Ill.: The Free Press, 1956).

12. See R. G. & V. Wasson, *Mushrooms, Russia, and History* (privately printed, 1957); R. G. Wasson, "The Hallucinogenic Fungi of Mexico," *Psychedelic Review*, 1, No. 1 (1963), pp. 27-42.

13. Aldous Huxley, *The Doors of Perception* (New York: Harper and Row, 1954).

14. Valuable information of events leading to, but not including the dismissal controversy itself, may be found in T. Leary, *High Priest* (Cleveland: World Publishing, 1968). My personal knowledge of the events consisted of participation in seminars organized for professors and scholars of religion by Dr. Leary dating from late 1961; involvement as an organizer and director in the affairs of the International Federation for Internal Freedom; assistance with the Good Friday Experiment; extensive follow-up of the Concord Prison Project, and

warm personal friendship and respect for Dr. Leary, which I still re-
tain. At one time or another I have been swayed by and weighed all
of the conflicting positions aroused by the controversy. Recently I have
taken the trouble to review the facts with Dr. Leary, as well as with
certain involved representatives of other positions. I have found him
amazingly without rancor in his judgments of Harvard and helpful
in aiding me to clarify in my own mind for this book the picture of the
whole situation. My own approach to the drugs, which may differ from
his, can be judged by comparing this volume with his writings. We
concur in the desire for a continuation of the study of the drugs in
order to maximize their value to religion.

15. T. Leary, *High Priest,* pp. 2, 20. Leary's *Psychedelic Prayers*
(Kerhonkson, N.Y.: Poets Press, 1966) reveals genuine poetic insight
and gift of expression, which the reader may check for himself.

16. John Milton, *Paradise Lost,* Part 1.

17. I received this information from the office of the President of Harvard
University in a letter dated February 9, 1967, which was a response to
my inquiry. Dr. Farnsworth and Professor McClelland, in particular,
very kindly took time to discuss their recollections of the Leary incident with me, and I have tried to present their positions as fairly as I
can. Their views naturally differ from my own. Dr. Farnsworth was good
enough to supply the following statement relative to his position on the
Good Friday Experiment:

"By arrangement between the Dean of Harvard College and Mr. Leary
and his associates, the total supply of psilocybin in their possession
was to be given to me for safekeeping until the proper procedures
surrounding such research were worked out. Presumably, all interested
groups (Department of Social Relations, University Health Services,
Office of the Dean of Students, etc.) would be involved in developing
such procedures. When, a few days later, I was asked to release the
drug before policies governing its use had been worked out, I did not
do so for obvious reasons. When I heard a few days later that the
Good Friday experiment at the Boston University Chapel had been
carried out on schedule, I was left to draw my own conclusions. Not
until this year did I learn the source of the psilocybin that was used."

In Leary's book, *The Politics of Ecstasy* (New York: G. P. Putnam's
Sons, 1968), p. 237, a lecture at Central Washington State College
states, "This is my last lecture as a college teacher to a college audience.
. . ." The note states that the lecture was delivered a week before he

was fired from Harvard. Its title was, "American Education as an Addictive Process and its Cure." It may have been this statement, or a similar one at Los Angeles, that prompted the phone call from the reporter to Dr. McClelland.

18. William James, *The Varieties of Religious Experience*, p. 292.

19. *Ibid.*

20. *Ibid.*

21. William Ernest Hocking, *The Meaning of God in Human Experience* (New Haven: Yale University Press, 1912), p. 349.

22. See W. H. McGlothlin, *Hippies and Early Christianity* (Institute of Government and Public Affairs, MR-101, University of California, Los Angeles, 1967).

23. In one hundred replies to a questionnaire I have circulated among psychedelic drug users, only one has stated he was sorry to have taken psychedelics in the first place, though he specifically stated that they had done him no harm. This has confirmed my more informal impressions covering some two hundred additional drug users. So far there is *not one* who has not described some element of religious experience on the questionnaire.

5. Religion and Ecstasy

One may say truly . . . that personal religious experience has its root and centre in mystical states of consciousness.
—William James[1]

By this time, the reader to whom psychedelic or hallucinogenic drugs conjured up the specter of poisonous substances that drive men mad, will sense that the situation is considerably more complex than this. Some states of mind induced by the drugs come very close to paralleling the profound experiences characteristic of those whom tradition has marked as among the very greatest exponents of our religious traditions. In the last chapter I noted, not only recent scientific rediscovery of the properties of these drugs, but their effects on certain individuals who thereafter have behaved *like* religiously motivated persons, in the past and present. Their religious behavior has been ratified by their insistence on their rght to use these drugs religiously, and it has been confirmed by their willingness to accept jail sentences, rejection by society and other harassments in their pursuit of the discovery of themselves.

This chapter will discuss the place of ecstasy in religion to supply a framework which will allow us to consider what place, if any, drug-induced ecstasy may have in contemporary religious life.

Three Modern Religious Trends. Modern religious movements have shown at least three important and somewhat contradictory trends. The first is the traditional western emphasis on rationality, pointed out in the first chapter. This is most visible in the science of theology, where consistent and logical conceptualization of religion has occurred, built in varying degrees on reason, dogma or faith. Yet, one can detect in the pages of such theologians as Paul Tillich and Karl Barth notes of the numinous, or the nonrational. These references are not so clearly seen in the pages of their disciples. The attempt to reconcile science and religion by imposing scientific rubrics on religion is less influential, but it is part of the rationalizing spirit. This movement has partly failed, because it has tended to be inhospitable to the categories of theology and unwilling to accept the preconceptions and structures upon which theology has built. Often each camp has insisted upon its own particular dogmas, and their intransigence has prevented true dialogue, though it is true that science, for example, in the Heisenburg principle of quantum physics, has grown less positivistic and deterministic than it once was, and so has been able to come closer to an understanding of religion.

A still more important movement has been toward the secularization of religion. Examples of this trend may be found in the writings of Harvey Cox, as well as in the "death of God" theologians. In general, the movement is away from the emphasis on the transcendent and the sacred in religion and toward the finding of values in the "worldly" life. Thomas Altizer speaks of God's giving up his transcendent majesty. In this sense, God is "willing his own death" in order to become immanent and incarnate.[2] It would seem obvious that the phrase "death of God" is used chiefly for its shock value. "Transformation of God" would be a better term, or rather "transformation in what people consider religion." Some of these writers, like Cox himself, have grown recently in coming to terms with the area of the sacred.

A third generalized movement focuses on the cultivation of the inner life in response to the hunger for expression of the nonrational aspects of the psyche. In the secular area this commonly appears in new forms of music, art, poetry and dance. Its religious expression, as I have said before, is mysticism, prophecy, speaking in tongues and other forms of religious ecstasy. The interest in Zen, certain aspects of the liturgical movement and Pentecostalism are varied expressions of the nonrational in religion. Certain religiously oriented hippie communities, reminiscent to some degree of the early Franciscans and medieval monastic communities, share this same impulse.

Of these three trends, the drug movement clearly belongs with the last. Rationalist intellectuals tend to scorn the psychedelic experience as antagonistic to clear thinking, if not a flight into delirium. Secularists deplore the fact that often the LSD intoxicated person reports an experience of the sacred or the holy, which they see as turning back history and the march of progress. Derisively used, the term "dropout" too easily comes to their lips. They assume that the user of the psychedelic drugs immediately deserts activities that improve society in favor of a chronic "contemplation of his navel." But someone who has long been fed on the husks of religious dogma, and who hungers for more vital encounter with God, or Ultimate Reality, or the Ground of Being, or whatever he may call the source of the movement which he intuitively feels will stir the deepest chords within himself, cannot be satisfied with a mere counsel of activism. He cannot be satisfied, because his drug-induced religious experience vitalizes his religious life and demonstrates the error of those who think that only the logical and rational aspects of religion are valid. His revitalized religious life vividly shows the secularists who say, "God is dead!" that God is not dead to them; he is alive and close to them.

The Nature and Importance of Mysticism. Religious ecstasy is the very core of religion as far as its personal forms go. William James wrote, "One may say truly, I think, that personal religious

experience has its root and centre in mystical forms of consciousness."[3] Any discussion, however, as to what religion is must
begin with the admission that there is no hope that we will
ever come to a general consensus. Any unabridged dictionary, as
noted previously, will disclose a dozen or more definitions,
some of them contradictory. Any person's definition is more likely
to throw light on himself than on any supposedly objective
category of reference. I presented my own definition in the first
chapter and pointed out there that it leaned in the direction of
mysticism. Despite the fact that it represents only *one way* of
conceiving religion, I think there are good reasons for using
mysticism as a basic concept in the defining of the religious
self.[4]

The chief advantage of this definition is that the mystical
consciousness is so different from other forms of consciousness
that it can be clearly distinguished from them. Other aspects
of religion have counterparts in the secular. Thinking and rationalizing may concern religion or something else; morality may
exist—as it often does—completely apart from a religious meta-
physic; the struggle for civil rights and social righteousness is
not of necessity religious. On the other hand, institutionalism
and the drive for power are as prevalent in the church as in
secular organizations. Of course, many religious apologists wel-
come these facts as an indication that religion is no longer
cloistered. It is vital and growing. This is the goal of the religious
secularizers. That any activity should be recognized as religious,
and *nothing other than religious,* seems to them an anachronism
as well as evidence that religion has withdrawn from life and will
wither.

The concept of religion as mysticism, or vivid inner experience
of Ultimate Reality, prevents it from becoming sterile. It is
significant that those who have been surprised by a mystical
experience seldom fail to feel that their experience is religious.

Intuitively they become aware—at least subjectively—that their state of mind somehow links them with the saints and prophets of the ages. This is the case even with atheists resistant to the thought that they have been in the presence of God.

A beautiful illustration of this, unconnected with any drug, is to be found in the autobiographical account of Arthur Koestler, *The Invisible Writing*, in the chapter, "The Hours by the Window." As a Communist and a doctrinaire atheist, he awaited execution in a Spanish prison. The contemplation of a mathematical problem suddenly triggered a mystical experience of great depth during which he felt "dissolved" in "the universal pool" and experienced "the peace that passeth understanding." As a result, he felt "drained of all tension" and "like an old car with its batteries freshly recharged," quite ready for a profound change of personality and values, which subsequently occurred. But he "also liked to think that the founders of religions, prophets, saints and seers, had at moments been able to read a fragment of the invisible text . . ."

Rudolf Otto has made this same point in *The Idea of the Holy* when he describes the experience of the holy as completely unique. W. T. Stace, though not completely agreeing with Otto about the phenomenon he is describing, has isolated seven characteristics as "the universal core" of mysticism. Every person who has a genuine mystical experience reports that he sees the unity, reality and infinity in space and time of all creation. He feels joy, peace and a sense of the sacred. He knows that his experience is true, although it may be paradoxical. Above all, his experience is indescribable.[5]

The average religious scholar dismisses mysticism as esoteric, if not positively harmful and dangerous. Therefore, it would seem too narrow a concept to deserve a place at the center of a definition of religion. Yet this is certainly not the subjective feeling of the mystic. He is likely to feel, as Koestler did, that this gift had lain fallow all of his life; that it was a writing in invisible ink whose rubrics he had previously glimpsed, though never so clearly.

What dictates my emphasis is in part the belief that we all share this potentiality, and that it influences us whether we know it or not. It requires only a subtle pattern of circumstance for it to appear before our consciousness in all its richness. Furthermore, as Stace points out in the last chapter of *Mysticism and Philosophy*, mysticism may be the ultimate source of ethics, morality and the life of righteousness. The lives of Francis of Assisi, Teresa of Avila, the Buddha, Loyola, Fox, Woolman, Swedenborg, Pascal and hosts of other mystics show clearly that their mystical and ecstatic religious experiences were the sources of their astonishing vitality and efficiency in pursuit of good works. Koestler's mystical experience, for example, changed his personality and motivated his withdrawal from Communist activities. Physicians and psychologists have grossly neglected this force that can make the pious promises of ecclesiastical faith come true.

Mysticism in Perspective. But if mysticism is as important as this, we must acknowledge that its role is to be the seed, or the leaven in the loaf. As a meal of leaven would be tasteless, even revolting, so religion composed exclusively of mysticism would be a cultural mistake. In order to put mysticism in perspective it helps to consider four religious types, all of whom are necessary in some degree to the full flowering of traditional religion. They are the priest, the prophet, the religious intellectual and the mystic.[6]

The most visible of these four types is the priest, essentially conservative, who represents the religious institution in its tradition, ceremonies and discipline. Closely related to the priest is the religious intellectual, usually the theologian. He is often closely related to the priest in that he supplies the conceptual framework around which the church, the religious institution, operates. The theologian through the ages has supplied the rationalizations to justify the harassment and burning of heretics. The theologian has also beaten new conceptual paths and so contributed to the intellectual ferment which has always played a part in the church's progress.

Standing against the priest, and to some extent the religious intellectual, have been the children of ecstasy, the prophet and the mystic. Both of these take their inspiration, not primarily from logic, tradition or institutions, but from powerful interior urges. The prophet is immersed in history and, like Amos and Isaiah, sees God's purposes in terms of morality and righteousness. "Thus saith the Lord!" is the ancient formula that expresses the consuming fire within the consciousness of the prophet. Many prophets have also been mystics. Isaiah's prophetic mission began with his vision of God and the cherubim. But where the prophet tends to see righteousness as the end of his mission, the mystic counts good works simply the by-product of his vision. The immediate experience of the One and the Holy is the supreme gift to the creature. It makes love, and the deeds associated with it, an effortless joy.

In reality, none of these is a pure type. The complete religious person possesses varying proportions of these components. Each has its important function in the religious enterprise and within the individual. Some religious persons display these components in nice balance, but most, including the outstanding personalities of religious history, develop one or another disproportionately.

Any one of these four facets of religion may overreach itself and need correction by one or more of the other three. Fanaticism, the sickness of the ecstatic, is balanced by the critical faculty of the intellectual or the appeal to tradition of the priest. The priest is subject to what William James, in *The Varieties*, called "religion's wicked practical partner, the spirit of corporate dominion," and the theologian may consort with "religion's wicked intellectual partner, the spirit of dogmatic dominion."[7]

When religion has threatened to become an empty institutional shell shored up by dessicated theological concepts, both prophet and mystic have clothed the dry bones of the church with the flesh of living religion. More even than the prophet, the mystic has reached down to a source that at one time seems to be nothing more than his essential self, and at another a transcendental and boundless sea of no time and no space constituting that "dark silence" of which van Ruysbroeck spoke wherein "all lovers lose themselves," until one flees "into the wild Sea, whence no created thing can draw us back again."[8]

The man who catches a glimpse of this vision, even only momentarily, seldom doubts that he has reached a realm of truth that takes precedence over every other thing. This is "the pearl of great price," which is "more precious than rubies"; this is the moment when the scales fall from our eyes so that finally we may see. So speaks the inward voice. Toward the end of his life, St. Thomas Aquinas experienced the ecstatic consciousness. He declared that this moment made all his writings "like straw."[9]

Mysticism as a Way of Perceiving the World. One of the points around which this discussion revolves is that mysticism is the profoundest and most essential function of the human spirit (the human "psyche" or the human "personality," if one prefers terms more congenial to the psychologists). Out of mysticism prophecy, then theology and finally religious institutions develop. The last is little more than a hollow shell, the theologian who serves it little more than a player of games with artificial rules, unless his "game" is in some way geared to the immediate and transcendent vision of God, the Ultimate, which underlies all nature and all culture. Civilization itself is also dependent on religion in this essential sense. As all science is dependent on nature, and all wholesome living on man's knowing who he is, so healthy civilization is dependent on the cosmic poet who points the way toward that well of instruction by which to live, the mystical consciousness. It was a mystic who exhorted us not to seek to inquire for whom the bell tolls, because it tolls for us. It was the mystic Gandhi who engineered one of the most successful revolutions in all of history; while Plato held that the leader who had not been illuminated was not fit to rule the state.

Unless the statesmen of mighty nations, the proud commanders of shining armaments, somehow absorb this wisdom, then civilization will become a shambles. Indeed, ominous warnings of the approach of the latter can hardly escape any twentieth-century man.

It is important, therefore, that we be as clear as possible about this elusive state of mind, this "mystical consciousness." It is usually thought of as a state of considerable vagueness, if not confusion, an emotion that addles the brain, deludes the subject and confounds any business influenced by it. In academic circles there is hardly a more cutting comment than to brand an opponent "mystical."

I have already, by referring to the studies of W. T. Stace, given a phenomenological description of the mystical state. But it is necessary to emphasize that the mystical consciousness is not primarily an emotion; it is a *perception*. Furthermore, this perception is not hazy, vague and confused. It is, particularly in its most distinguished exponents, remarkably simple, cogent and clear.

What does one mean when he speaks of a "perception"? It may help to present a simple series of illustrations to bring the word into context and so illuminate further the term "mysticism."

One enters a dimly lit room and notices a coiled object in the corner. One sees it to be a coiled rope. This recognition is a "perception," probably to be dismissed with little or no response as one goes about his business. But this perception may change with closer scrutiny, and one may see the object as a coiled cobra. Immediately the perceiver's emotions are aroused. The emotion is closely associated with the perception, and yet is distinct from it. The emotion might disorganize the observer leading him, in his fright, to confused and even foolish acts. But it would be the very cogency and clarity of the initial perception that would lead to his sharp and disorganized reactions as he seeks either to flee from or to kill the snake.

Let us take the illustration another stage and suppose the perceiver a truly pious Hindu, informed not only by the letter of his beliefs but by actual and immediate perception of the eternal Unity, the experience to which mystics universally testify. He will perceive not only a cobra. Even in his terror and dread, he will perceive a fellow creature with which he must dwell despite mortal danger. He will no more think of killing this creature than he would consider cutting off one of his own hands. In a peculiarly cogent sense this would be a religious or mystical perception, and the encounter with the cobra would be transformed from a frightening trauma into a religious experience. To us, this reaction of the Hindu may seem like the merest folly. But it illustrates how the strange alchemy of mystical experience may enable an individual to "love his enemy." It also shows that the essential principle of mysticism is perception, even though usually accompanied by strong emotion, which the uninformed may mistake for the perception itself. With a marvelous Franciscan cogency and clarity often combined with a startling suddenness, the mystic *perceives* all things as *one,* all men as his brothers, all creatures as his fellows and all matter holy. It is no wonder that a mystical vision marks a sharp change in behavior.

Mysticism and Society. This transforming and enabling function of the mystical consciousness lends it importance. To perceive a cobra as a fellow may seem the height of sentimental rashness, yet there are cases on record where those attuned to the natural world have "tamed" wild beasts and serpents, too. Cases have been reported of those who have tamed deadly rattlesnakes with love.[10] Martin Buber extended his "I-Thou" relationship to the trees and the falling rain.[11] It was reputed that St. Francis, besides identifying himself with the light and warmth of the sunlight, held converse with the birds and made a companion of the savage Brother Wolf.

Rather than superciliously pass over accounts of these strange feats as fables, achievements by the abnormally gifted, or illustrations of non-drug-assisted "freak-outs," it is wise to examine the values of such gifts more thoroughly. Such an examination may teach us how to avoid danger from our fellow mortals, often deadlier than cobras! For what else than cobras, boa constrictors and wolves in human form are such varying figures as Dostoevsky's Grand Inquisitor, Hitler, Stalin or the general who uses napalm bombs on villages filled with innocent children? If the beasts of the field may be subdued and made responsive by a man who has experienced the unity of all things in mystical vision, perhaps even an apparently stony-hearted human being has a tender spot through which another, properly oriented through a religious experience, may reach him. The dogs of war, only precariously chained now, may be kept in check to prevent a lethal scramble for political and dogmatic dominion. It would be naive for us to expect that a sudden encounter with mysticism would shortly solve all the world's problems. But a glance at mysticism will uncover aspects of life that offer some promise.

Some claim, and others vigorously deny, that psychedelic drugs have triggered genuine religious experience of a profound and transforming nature in many persons. Is this experience the same as the mystical experience just mentioned? If the perceptions touched off by the drugs are in any reliable sense religious, then an invaluable means of studying the dynamics and effects of profound religious experience at firsthand is available to us. If this is the case, then there may also be available to us a means of vitalizing religion and multiplying its benefits, perhaps on a small scale, as seems to be the case with the Native American Church, but perhaps on a very much larger scale. We should not allow our imaginations to run away with us, however. There are many pitfalls and difficulties in the way. New discoveries often make even the scientific mind sanguine, so we must be critical. But we know how timid, smug and unprogressive people can be— even the scientists. So it is necessary for us to be bold. In the next chapter it will be our task to consider more thoroughly whether, in good conscience, we may consider the effects of the drugs as religious.

NOTES

1. William James, *The Varieties of Religious Experience* (New York: New American Library, 1958), p. 292.
2. See T. J. J. Altizer, *The Gospel of Christian Atheism* (Philadelphia: Westminster Press, 1966). For a good journalistic account of the death of God movement, see W. Braden, *The Private Sea: LSD and the Search for God* (Chicago: Quadrangle Books, 1967), chap. 10.
3. W. James, *Varieties*, p. 292.
4. W. H. Clark, "Mysticism as a Basic Concept in Defining the Religious Self," *Lumen Vitae*, 19 No. 2 (1966), pp. 231-232.
5. See W. T. Stace, *Mysticism and Philosophy*, chap. 2.
6. For a fuller description of these types see W. H. Clark, *The Psychology of Religion* (New York: Macmillan, 1958), chaps. 12-13.
7. W. James, *Varieties*, p. 263.
8. J. van Ruysbroeck in W. T. Stace, ed., *The Teachings of the Mystics* (New York: New American Library, 1960), p. 169.
9. G. K. Chesterton, *St. Thomas Aquinas* (New York: Doubleday, 1956), p. 143.
10. H. G. McCurdy, *The Personal World* (New York: Harcourt, Brace & World, Inc., 1961), p. 543.
11. See M. Buber, *I and Thou*, 2nd Edition (New York: Charles Scribner's Sons, 1958) and other volumes by Buber.

6. Association Between Drugs and Religion: Contemporary Investigations

I started the session in a twilight zone of prenatal memories. The fear of having to be reborn was followed by an overwhelming joy in being alive. I discovered, as if for the first time, the life of everything around and rejoiced in it. I experienced the awe and mystery of the creation of life, divining in each animate thing the atomic chaos from which it developed and to which it will return. I seemed to participate in the religious rite of the grasshoppers in the grass before me and through this became aware of the holiness of things. I sensed the presence of God! The experience was followed by an intense joy, coupled with loneliness and sorrow at my incapacity to fill others with the wonderment of being alive.

—adapted from an atheist's description of his LSD session

Though it has long been known to practitioners of religion that drugs, and other forms of biochemical intervention, like fasting, could facilitate religious experience, it is only recently that scientists and religious scholars have turned to studying the process in any systematic way. James mentions some of the earliest attempts in his *Varieties of Religious Experience*, particularly in his references to the writing of Benjamin Blood.[1] James had heard of the peyote ceremonies and had tried "mescal" himself, but the drug made him violently sick.[2] More successful was his experiment with nitrous oxide, which occupies a prominent place in the chapter on mysticism in *The Varieties of Religious*

Experience. The mystical strain in James' father, which William had never before quite understood, received startling confirmation. Because of this experiment, which was conducted several years before he delivered his famous Gifford lectures, James was convinced that the mystical consciousness is distinct from other forms of consciousness, and that it is the root of all religions. After an allusion to the mystical consciousness, he says:

> . . . our normal waking consciousness, rational consciousness as we call it, is but one special type of consciousness, whilst all about it, parted by the filmiest of screens, there lie potential forms of consciousness entirely different. . . . No account of the universe in its totalilty can be final which leaves these other forms of consciousness quite disregarded . . . they forbid a premature closing of our accounts with reality. Looking back on my own experiences, they all converge towards a kind of insight to which I cannot help ascribing some metaphysical significance.[3]

In 1953 Aldous Huxley, as described in Chapter 4, tried some mescaline and wrote an account of his experiment and reactions in *The Doors of Perception*. He recommended the drug as a safe road to mystical perceptions, the changes in personality that often accompany mysticism, and the vitalizing of religion for the average man. This essay was perhaps the first introduction to the general public of the subject of drugs as a legitimate road to the artistic and religious life. Huxley also pointed out that the stimulation of biochemical bodily changes as an element in the production of religious experience has been not only traditionally common but ecclesiastically approved. Fasting and special diets, both deliberate and inadvertent, have been factors in ecstasy.[4]

A reply to Huxley was not long in coming. R. G. Zachner, a Roman Catholic student of comparative religion and a professor at Oxford, unlike many critics of the drugs, decided to see for himself. He also took mescaline, but it did not impress him. There was nothing specifically Christian in it, he concluded, and it was nontheistic. He did acknowledge an experience of a natural mysticism, which he set on a much lower plane than the more orthodox and more religious variety. Both his experiment and his quarrel with Huxley are set forth in a scholarly volume, *Mysticism: Sacred and Profane,* which also includes much matter of more general interest.

The Good Friday Experiment. The most cogent single piece of evidence that psychedelic chemicals do, under certain circumstances, release profound religious experience, is the Good Friday Experiment. There are no experiments known to me in the history of the scientific study of religion better designed or clearer in their conclusions than this one, which is also a tribute to the value of these drugs as superlative means for the study of religious experience.

The experiment constituted the Harvard Ph.D. dissertation of Walter N. Pahnke, already the possessor of both an M.D. and a B.D. The subjects were twenty first-year Protestant theological students who had never experienced this type of drug and knew very little of the nature or importance of mystical experience, though some had had what they considered religious experiences. Nearly all were anxious to enrich their religious life experientially, though one of the experimental subjects admitted afterward that he wished to demonstrate that no religious experience could result from ingesting drugs. He alone made no religious preparation for the experiment, and he was the only one of those who got the drug who reported no evidences of mystical experience.

After screening and preparation, in a double blind design, (which means that neither experimenter nor subjects knew who received the drug until the study was completed and ready for final conclusions) ten were given thirty milligrams of psilocybin and ten a placebo in indistinguishable pill form. All twenty then attended a two and one-half-hour Good Friday service in a private college chapel. Recorded spoken reports and written reports were collected after the service. The results indicated a sharp differentiation between the two groups. As criteria for mystical experience, Pahnke used Stace's seven characteristics of the "universal core" of mysticism, mentioned above, with the addition of two other criteria, *transiency of the experience* and *persistent positive changes in attitude and behavior.* He then trained three judges, otherwise unconnected with the experiment, to recognize evidence of the nine criteria. These judges were given the data collected from the subjects, with no indication as to which group they represented, and asked to identify any evidence that the subjects were reporting mystical experience. Nine out of the ten of the experimental group reported unmistakable evidence of having experienced at least some of the mystical consciousness, most of them to a marked degree. Only one member of the control group—those who received the placebo—experienced mystical consciousness, and his experience was only minor. Statistical analysis suggested that were the experiment to be repeated with similar subjects, the chances that some of the principal results and conclusions would be confirmed was greater than 999 in 1,000! Social scientists usually consider a hypothesis proved if the certainty of their results reaches 99 in 100. The definiteness of results in this experiment, as measured by many of the items, went far beyond. If we assume the adequacy of Pahnke's criteria, it would seem most difficult, if not impossible, to escape the conservative conclusion that, *in proper circumstances and in certain people properly prepared, the psychedelic drugs have a strong tendency to release mystical experience.*

In view of the criticism that psychedelic drugs—and mysticism too—tend to cause people to "drop out" and escape the real business of life, Pahnke's last criteria is significant. The subjects believed that the Good Friday service was a helpful religious event, but those who had taken the drug were convinced of its value. Even after a six months' followup, the two groups could still be significantly distinguished. Examples of statements by the experimental subjects in answer to questions about the effects follow:

Very strong benefit: a profound recognition of the "mystical" in the full religious life—but this attitude seemed not as an escape from the world, rather giving me a greater sense of concern for the here and now.

Very strong benefit: a startling sensitivity to others—especially those with "problems."

Very strong benefit: a sense of "'call"—insofar as this means that the Word must be proclaimed to the "world"—not so much verbally as "existentially," and that somehow I must respond to this challenge, as it has appeared to me.

That these changes in attitude toward the subject's work in the world was rooted in vivid personal experience is illustrated by the following:

Very strongly beneficial: I have had a much greater degree of self-realization since Good Friday. By this I mean a greater certainty of being and becoming. Closely connected with this is the feeling of being a creature of purpose.

I feel that I have a greater realization of my motives that lie beyond my various actions. I do believe I have an awareness of the selfishness that underlies many of my actions. This realization has been met with attempts to cast this selfishness aside to go beyond it.

I have made reference to the joy I experienced when I came back to life since the Good Friday afternoon experience. At times I have

felt a joy at being alive and having real existence I do not believe I
have ever experienced it previous to Good Friday to the degree I did
then or to the degree I have since, even though I intellectually knew
of it.

Taken with other comments by the experimental subjects such
as "feeling in love and unity and love with mankind," one easily
catches accents which leave the impression of being in touch
with true mystics. Such experiences may enrich and illumine
theological concepts as well.[5]

The following is quoted from the account written at my request by a theological student who had received psilocybin ex-
perimentally in a hospital setting under permissive and open-
minded supervision. He was encouraged to prepare himself in
any way he wished. The result he described as a "bad trip," at
least in the beginning, when the sudden confrontation with his
unsuspected weaknesses, and paranoid ideas toward the medical
personnel had been frightening. Nevertheless, his feeling that
the whole experience would be "meaningful and constructive"
was reinforced when the staff and several subjects sat down to
share a meal.

It seemed to me to come the closest to a celebration of the Lord's
Supper as I could imagine. . . . It was the feeling of being lost in my
own problem world that had frightened me before this. . . . Much of
my life I have felt alone, but at this moment it seemed as if our fellowship was a clue to the fact that we are never completely abandoned
in this life if we truly seek meaningful relationships with other people
in a searching sense of sincere responsibility and mutuality.

One of the results of this experiment has been the heightened perception of the *imago dei* in my fellow human beings. I am attempting
to state in theological terms what I feel to be a very important aspect
of the greatest insight into the secrets of life that I know of. Today
I was in a restaurant in Boston called the English Tea Room. I was

sitting across the table from a gentleman who will be shortly cele-
brating his 93rd birthday. He was a total stranger to me until I asked
him what the secret to long life was. Now I perceived that this gentleman was a man of character and many rich experiences. He was able
to enter into a conversation with (a) woman, . . . also elderly,
as a result of my first question. I was amazed at the sacredness of
life in such a simple thing such as eating a meal in a public restaurant. My whole point is not to be found in some equation which
that man could give me but in the fact of our common bond in the
humanity of God. I say "of God" because I consider this encounter
to be "holy"; that is, something of which all men can be aware but in
which few people take the time to get involved . . . The potential for
a casual conversation about life is possible for any two human beings.
I am aware that each man on the street has some spark of the divine
that makes him something more than the stray dog that visits each
bush and tree with devotion and excitement.

A careful reading of the passage will disclose the agency of
the drug in stimulating dialogue between the theological concept
and common experience, which should be the function of all
vital theologizing. It also reveals the drug as a solvent of the
characteristic New England reserve that denies the sharing of
life's most poignant concerns.

Investigation at Norwich Hospital. Another study with which
I am even more intimately acquainted, since it was my own,
was reported by myself and Milton Raskin, M.D., the research
psychiatrist in charge of administering the drug.[6] The Worcester
Foundation for Experimental Biology accepted eight unselected
normal volunteers for an experiment at Norwich Hospital, Connecticut, to study several aspects of the effects of varying dosages
of LSD administered daily over periods up to 16 days. My part
in the total experiment was to study religious factors. About ten
months after the experiment was over, the subjects were asked to

compare their experiences under the drug with their normal states of consciousness according to a five-point scale, ranging from 0, "no different from normal," to 5, "beyond anything ever experienced or imagined." The subjects ranged in age from twenty-two to forty-two. Two were theological students and two were atheists. All were liberal, if not radical in their views toward religion. Their reactions on twenty dimensions are summarized in the accompanying table.

Inspection of the table will make it immediately apparent that all subjects, in varying degrees, reported aspects of religious and particularly mystical experience. The two atheists (K and M) were among the three reporting the most intense experience of a religious nature; one of the theological students (W) was the third. Though very resistant to the use of the term "God" in their reports at the time of the experiment, both atheists gave unmistakable evidence of intense religious natures by reporting experiences of "rebirth," "unity," "blessedness and peace," and "the Holy and the Divine." The patterns of the reported experience of no two subjects were exactly alike, but all subjects reported some measure of the heightening of their experience over normal in the areas of timelessness, unity and loss of the sense of self, unity with people, the Holy and the Divine, ineffability of the experience, fear and terror, mystery, esthetic experience and color.

The consensus, ten months later, was that the experience had had profound personal significance, five of the eight reporting it as "beyond anything ever experienced or imagined." Like the subjects in the Good Friday experiment, they felt that the experience had improved their capacity to deal realistically with their problems and had enormously stimulated their psychological growth. One of the subjects, a writer, discovered that he was no longer restricted in his writing to esoteric themes, where, with little research, he could easily become known as an expert.

SUBJECTIVE RATINGS OF FEELINGS BY SUBJECTS WITH VARYING DOSES OF LSD ON 9—11 MONTH FOLLOW-UP

DISTRIBUTION OF RATINGS

	0	1	2	3	4	5
Lower dosages	8	8	17	12	9	26
Higher dosages	6	1	6	19	16	26
Totals	17	9	26	31	25	52

	Subjects and Dosage in Mcgr. per Kilogram								Summary			
	K. 3.0	U. 3.0	M. 2.5	C. 2.5	W. 1.25	F. 1.25	Mc. .625	L. .625	Higher doses	Lower doses	Dif.	Average of Total
1. Timelessness	5	3	4.3	4	5	2	3	5	4.08	3.80	.28	3.94
2. Spacelessness	5	3	4.3	2.3	5	0	0	5	3.58	2.80	.78	3.19
3. Unity & Loss of Self	5	5	4.7	3	5	1	3	5	4.48	3.50	.58	3.89
4. Unity with Objects and Growing Things	0	4	2.7	2	4.3	2.3	0	1	2.18	1.82	.36	2.00
5. Unity with People	4	2	4.7	2	4	2	4	5	3.68	3.65	.03	3.66
6. Ultimate Reality	5	5	3.3	3.3	5	2.3	0	5	4.15	2.75	1.40	3.45
7. Blessedness and Peace	5	3	5	2.7	4.7	2.7	2.7	3	3.25	3.85	-.60	3.55
8. The Holy and Divine	5	4	4.3	4.3	5	2	3	5	4.15	3.68	.47	3.92
9. Paradoxicality	2	3	4.3	4.3	5	2.3	3	0	3.40	2.50	.90	2.95
10. Ineffability	5	3	4.3	3.5	5	2.7	3	1	3.15	3.82	-.67	3.45
11. Fear and Terror	5	5	4	3.5	5	2.7	2.7	0	4.12	2.35	1.77	3.23
12. Mystery	5	5	4.3	3.3	5	2.3	4	1	4.45	3.18	1.27	3.81
13. Joy	5	5	3.3	3.5	5	2.3	3	5	2.75	3.82	-1.07	3.29
14. Sense of Dying	0	2	0	0	5	2.3	1	5	1.65	2.32	-.67	1.99
15. Rebirth	1	0	4	3.3	5	0	4	0	2.00	3.32	-1.32	2.66
16. Presence of God	5	0	4	2	5*	2	1	5	2.25	3.25	-1.00	2.75
17. Esthetic Experience	5	3	4.7	3.3	5	1	4	1	4.00	4.00	.00	4.00
18. Color Intense	5	4	4.7	3.3	5	2	1	0	4.25	2.25	2.00	3.25
19. Music Moving	5	5	5	3	5	2	0	3	4.00	3.00	1.00	3.50
20. Significance of Experience	5	5	5	3	5	3	3	5	4.45	4.00	.45	4.22
Average of Total	4.15	2.70	4.23	2.62	4.70	1.70	2.40	3.53	3.50	3.18	.32	3.34

Scale 0 = normal state of mind; 1 = slightly above normal; 2 = clearly above normal; 3 = markedly and intensely above normal; 4 = exceedingly intense; 5 = beyond anything ever experienced or imagined.

He found himself writing in fields of more general interest, even in the area of history and religion. This was a development that, previous to LSD, he would have found unthinkable. His interests and his self-confidence had been enlarged. The reader may examine the table for himself and then decide whether or not there is strong evidence for the presence of profound religious experience.

An interesting sidelight on the investigation suggests that the fruits of drug-induced religion parallel what are considered the more normal variety. One of the characteristics of the civilized man most valued by society is the quality of compassion. All men wish to be understood, hence the intuitive attraction of others to the compassionate person. Not only is compassion supposed to be an element of religion, but one of the severest and most valid tests to which we can submit a man's religion is to ask whether or not it promotes and produces compassion. A prime element in the charisma of St. Francis, it is the characteristic most often cele- brated in references to Gautama, known as the *compassionate* Buddha, while prostitutes, publicans and sinners were attracted to Jesus because *they knew He would understand them.*

The second subject quoted in connection with the Good Friday experiment and the report of the theological student given psilo- cybin in a hospital illustrate that sensitivity to others and their problems was stimulated by the drug. Although it is not an in- variable accompaniment of the psychedelic experience, it has fre- quently been noted, for example in Chapter 4 of *The Varieties of Psychedelic Experience* by Masters and Houston, that empathy often does result from psychedelic experiences. It grows naturally out of the experience of unity. If one identifies himself with all things, it follows that he feels at one with his fellow creatures and so acknowledges responsibility toward them. It will be noted by reference to the above table that all the subjects reported an increased feeling of unity with people. The outstanding feature of the religious philosophy of Albert Schweitzer was reverence for life in all forms. This attitude characterizes Hinduism and Buddhism more explicitly than Western religions. An interesting and significant commentary on the experience of two of our subjects is that they found it impossible to kill even noxious insects for several months after their experience.

There is not space for recording all of the evidence supporting the association of the psychedelic experience with religious experience, but a sampling of examples may be found in studies by Masters and Houston, Leary, McGlothlin, Ditman, Savage, Huston Smith and in the volumes edited by Abramson.[8]

The Peyote Religion. One of the most instructive phenomena involving psychedelic drugs is the full-blown religious movement among American Indians institutionalized as the Native American Church. Information about this remarkable cult comes to us chiefly through researches of anthropologists such as Aberle, Slotkin, LaBarre and Castaneda.[9] Practices have probably descended from Aztec tradition, but the peyote religion, though built around the ingestion of this drug, nevertheless is a syncretic blend of Aztec and Christian elements with an admixture of what white Americans consider superstition and folklore.

Taken in sufficient quantities, peyote yields an experience very much like that mediated by LSD. The Indians either chew an appropriate quantity of the dried buttons or brew a bitter tea from them. This is taken at the beginning of a dignified night-long ceremony, usually in a tepee, with a priest or "road-chief" in charge, who directs the ceremony, assisted by lesser functionaries who drum, help in the hymn singing and tend the fire and the floor. Worshippers see visions and participate in experiences which draw the group together and facilitate adherence to the church's teachings. The religion has been growing among the Indians for several centuries. It has gained a foothold in nearly all the American and Canadian tribes, despite legal harassment and persecution from Indian agents and Christian missionaries, as well as opposition within the Indian communities themselves. In the nineteenth century bands of cultists began to coalesce into churches for protective purposes. At present the Native American Church comprises nearly all the worshippers. It is a loose federation of small worship communities variously estimated at from 30,000 to 250,000 members.[10] While whites have been admitted to the church, they have not ordinarily been encouraged to apply. Consequently only the anthropologists and a few rare guest, who have won the confidence of the Indians, have been admitted to the ceremonies.

Despite opposition, or perhaps because of it, the peyote religion has steadily increased its influence over the years and seems to be spreading. Peyotists generally consider themselves Christians, and they emphasize an ethic of brotherly love, family responsibility, self-reliance, hard work and avoidance of alcohol.[11] The most recent anthropological study of peyotism carefully concludes, in part, as follows:

The Native American Church of North America has proved itself to be a durable movement of great vitality, whose spread to new Indian groups continues today. . . . At present there is no evidence of addiction to peyote, or any satisfactory evidence of harm from it or physical benefit from it. Testimony amply supports the existence of feelings of spiritual, physical, and psychological benefit in most cases. . . .

No evidence has been discovered that supports the interpretation that the practices of the Native American Church of North America, including its use of Peyote, have damaging effects on the health, welfare, or morality of its members. Much evidence has been discovered that indicates that members of the Native American Church are seriously and strongly committed to their religion, including use of peyote, and if necessary they will suffer imprisonment rather than abandon the church and will fight cases through the courts, whether Tribal, State, or Federal, so long as they experience legal restriction.[12]

Students of church history will recognize in this account that these devoted Indians share the characteristics of religious separatists through the ages: the Qumran community, the followers of John the Baptist, Jesus and the Twelve, the early Christians, Francis and his followers; the Albigenses, Waldenses, Lollards, and the followers of Hus, Lutherans and Anabaptists; followers of the ecstatic Ignatius, the early Quakers and the Methodists, Hasidic communities of central Europe; and the Jehovah's Witnesses and the Amish of our own day. Beyond the Judeo-Christian tradition one might mention the followers of Socrates, the disciples of Gautama, many a Hindu Ashram, Zen communities, and Sufi movements. All these groups caused trouble for religious authorities and often civil authorities as well. Some have been benighted and extreme; but all, in one way or another, have discovered within themselves that universal river of ecstasy from which flowed the energy, power and refreshment to revive religious bodies tired out by too much intellectualism, moralism and institutionalism. An integral part of the cultic ecstasy of the peyote Indians and an unmistakable evidence of an intense religious life is their willingness to defy the law and to endure harassment and persecution rather than give up what to them is central in their religious practices.

The peyote cult helps to establish a perspective on contemporary drug problems concerned with psychedelics. Doctors, magistrates, legislators and the general public support their attitudes with the fiction that the psychedelics are ingested only by frivolous and rebellious youth, the sole substantial result being the risk of mental illness and perhaps death. Such undiscriminating and one-sided views have resulted in jail and ruined careers for hundreds of refined and religiously sensitive young people. Worse than this, many a parent has been alienated from sons and daughters who conclude from their own experience with the drugs that tragedy is rare, and religious and artistic growth is frequent. It has resulted in a large, inchoate, underground

religious movement involving the drugs that has become dangerous at times largely because of the hiatus between parent and
child, between laws and practice.

The peyote Indians have survived the period in which the
ingestion of peyote made them felons, and they now have
generally established their legal right to use peyote sacramentally.
Their capacity to use a psychedelic drug without abuse not only
inheres in certain properties of these drugs, but more importantly
in the cooperation of a tradition and legal system that has finally
operated to allow their usage. The religious structure safeguards
participants at the same time that it helps direct the energies the
drugs release into creative and socially wholesome channels. The
peyotists have demonstrated that the drugs may facilitate a
viable religious movement. They also teach white authorities how
much more rationally the Indians handle a psychedelic drug in
the interest of religion and responsible living.

Regardless of the final disposition of the drugs as a factor in
religious life, it would seem difficult for the responsible church
member to dismiss such testimony as irrelevant and frivolous.
The churches can neglect such evidence only on the peril that a
cogent agent of religious life may be rejected and be left to
cultists, some of whom may use the drugs irresponsibly and some
in such a way as to throw discredit on the churches themselves.
The latter may appear to mediate a religious life of such superfici-
ality that their spiritual influence may further dwindle. History
bears ample testimony that this has happened before. The average
church will tend to reject any discussion of the drugs that does
not damn them. But the challenge for the church is to face
courageously *all* aspects of the question with open-mindedness
before making a premature judgment.

Do the Drugs Cause Religious Experience? An important
theoretical and practical issue is whether or not the drugs *cause*
religious experience. This does not follow simply because the

two are associated. The observant reader will have noted that I tend to use the terms *release* or *trigger* religious experience, though there is no doubt that the drugs may in a sense be a part of a complex of factors that help us to explain a marvelous, captivating and mystery-producing encounter with what some of us call Ultimate Reality, others the Creator and still others simply God.

The reason I prefer the term *release* rather than *cause* is not that the drugs are the only road to religious experience or even the best road, but that millions of Americans will attain religious experience through the drugs or not at all. Nature, liturgies, sensory deprivation, disciplined meditation, the dance, music, Bible reading, preaching, loving acts and many other conditions, either singly or in myriad combinations, may help to open the doors. Like sensitivity to beauty, the capacity to encounter the Holy seems to reside within every human soul. Too often it may sleep there eternally, but it is ready to be awakened by the right combination of circumstances.

The drugs do not produce anything that is not already there, nor must people get the idea that they can create intelligence out of dullness, as some may imply. Just as photographic chemicals bring to light the picture already imprinted on the film, the psychedelic chemicals have, in actual practice, introduced many people to an appreciation for music, a capacity for art or a sensitivity to poetry that was there but which they never dreamed they had. It has been the function of this chapter to present some of the evidence that these chemicals can act as an Aladdin's lamp to raise, out of the depths of the self, the genius for knowing the Holy, the awesome knowledge that the stuff of which we are made is also Divine.

Summary. To summarize the chapter, we may say that William James and Aldous Huxley are not the only ones who have suggested that religious states of mind may be triggered through the agency of drugs. Careful and systematically carried out investigations, like the Good Friday Experiment, have clearly demonstrated that experiences of a religious and ecstatic nature have been so released. In a much wider area, anthropologists have studied the peyote cult among the American Indians and have reported favorably on its influence. The Indians' willingness to suffer imprisonment and persecution in defense of their right to use peyote reinforces the impression of their sincerity and the fact that peyotism is truly religious. A study of the Native American Church has much to teach the white community in the way of understanding and directing religious energies released by the drugs. On the basis of the evidence the conclusion would seem inescapable that an important property of the psychedelic chemicals is their agency as a releaser of profound religious experience of an ecstatic and mystical nature in many persons who otherwise would never dream that they had the capacity.

NOTES

1. W. James, *Varieties,* chapter on mysticism.
2. G. W. Allen, *William James* (New York: Viking Press, 1967), p. 383.
3. *Varieties,* p. 298. See opening paragraph of the chapter on mysticism for James' view of the importance of the subject to religion.
4. Aldous Huxley, *The Doors of Perception* and *Heaven and Hell* (New York: Harper & Row, 1964), pp. 145-156.
5. I assisted at the Good Friday Experiment, and I knew and talked to all twenty subjects. Those for whom Dr. Pahnke's thesis is unavailable will find a summary in his chapter in the Abramson volume listed in the bibliography, or in W. N. Pahnke and W. A. Richards, "Implications of LSD and Experimental Mysticism," *Journal of Religion and Health,* 3 (July, 1966), pp. 175-208. Quotations are from the Thesis.
6. Clark and Raskin, "LSD As a Means of Exploring the Nonrational Components of the Religious Consciousness" (Paper presented at the Annual Meeting of the Society for the Scientific Study of Religion, Atlanta, Georgia, October 27, 1967). Thanks for cooperation are also due to collaborators, Drs. J. Bergen, W. Koella, and D. Krus.

7. W. H. Clark and M. Raskin, Table, "Subjective Ratings of Feelings by Subjects with Varying Doses of LSD."

8. Most of these investigators cited in Masters and Houston, *The Varieties of Psychedelic Experience*, chap. 9. The Abramson volumes will be referred to in the following chapter.

9. R. C. DeBold and R. C. Leaf, *LSD, Man and Society* (Middletown, Conn.: Wesleyan University Press, 1967), pp. 75-76, 104-108.

10. J. S. Slotkin, *The Peyote Religion* (Glencoe, Ill.: Free Press, 1956), pp. 60-71.

11. *Ibid.*

12. David F. Aberle, *The Peyote Religion Among the Navaho* (Chicago: Aldine Publishing Company, 1966); copyright © 1966 by Wenner-Gren Foundation for Anthropological Research, Inc., pp. 352-354.

7. Drugs and Personality Change

Quarry the granite rock with razors, or moor the vessel with a thread of silk; then you may hope with such keen and delicate instruments as human knowledge and human reason to contend against these giants, the passion and the pride of man.
—John Henry Cardinal Newman[1]

All my life came before my eyes and I said, "What a waste!"
—An armed robber's report on his drug session

Such psychedelic experiences seem to have a powerful effect and can so change a person's attitude toward life that he will give up forever his maladaptive responses in favor of a healthier point of view.
—Ruth Fox, M.D.[2]

Can drugs effect constructive personality change? The spontaneous response of the average citizen to this question will be, "No." He will think of the pitiable derelicts brought to their condition through addiction to heroin. But the idea that drugs might be used to enhance life and to integrate personality is so foreign to his habitual way of thinking that he will reject it as absurd, if not dangerous and repulsive. The way to combat passion and human frailty is obviously through intelligence and will power!

This chapter will concentrate on this issue of the psychedelics and personality change. I will try to demonstrate that, carefully used by trained and experienced experts, the psychedelic drugs actually have been influential in such beneficent changes in many people. Furthermore, I will show that constructive and lasting changes have often been associated with stressful and awesome experiences described as religious by the subjects, as in the case of the armed robber recounted in the first pages of this volume and quoted in the heading of this chapter.

In the last chapter I presented evidence that the "psychedelic" or "mind revealing" experience frequently demonstrated that men are fundamentally religious, and the experiences released by the intoxication are indistinguishable from religious experiences triggered by more traditional methods. In my account of the experiments, I have already anticipated some material which I will propose with increased rigor here.

At the outset of my discussion I wish to review briefly certain truths about religious experience. First of all, I repeat my assertion that profound religious experience is *always* moving and probably the most captivating and shattering experience known to man. When I say "shattering" I mean that the experience shatters certain fundamental assumptions about life which stand in the way of a broader and more humane view. This "shaking of the foundations" sharply distinguishes the intensely religious person from the generality of society and explains why he is often seen by his fellows as a radical or eccentric. What we call "respectability," whether in church or in secular society, serves in part to protect social and ecclesiastical institutions from the explosive influence of the prophet and the mystic. But it also blocks the individual from that radical reordering of his personality variously referred to as "salvation," "redemption," or "rebirth" to the degree that these terms have psychological and behavioral significance. It saves him from stress and wins for him, not the "peace that passes understanding," but the comfort that resides in the commonplace. The latter is the reward of caution and reason. The former is the child of ecstasy.

Written large on the pages of history are such examples of this truth as Socrates, Gautama, St. Francis, and Jesus, all of whom had some friction with their families and society. A more modern instance is the painter, Vincent Van Gogh. A basically religious sudden insight in his early career indicated that following Jesus Christ did not involve him in the family pattern of success and the securing of a theological degree but rather in identification with underprivileged and exploited miners, even to living, like them, in a miserable shack and sharing with them coarse food and rough clothing until he was close to starvation. Such devotion was unacceptable to his family and to the religious societies who might have supported him. It was typical of his ecstatic and passionate nature that this and subsequent changes in insights and orientations came to him suddenly and as revelations. In a sense, these changes were only variations in a passionate personality that stayed the same; in another sense, each one made him a new man and radically changed his way of life.[3] Civilization is the richer for the lives of each one of these ecstatics. But the "new man" that each became made him a trial to his family and a stumbling block to his neighbors.

It is this kind of rebirth that we must look for as the result of the psychedelic experience, if I am further to support my contention of the last chapter that these experiences are truly religious. In this chapter I will try to cite evidence that in specific problem areas the ecstatic experience may shatter the appearance of the commonplace and create the "new man" who, hitherto inept, can now master himself and express that which impels his inner self toward his destiny. "Destiny" in this sense is to be sharply distinguished from the humdrum economic and social activities that must be the duty of every mortal, but which so possess the average man that he completely identifies his aims with those about him, and becomes "other-directed."

But the prophet, the artist, the mystic and the poet, in those moments when they are most fully and intensely themselves, find their direction deeply and uniquely within themselves at a depth to illuminate them with a cosmic wisdom that binds them to all humanity. This wonderful gift, residing potentially within all of us, disturbs even the most conventional citizen with a restlessness and a malaise that only the most frenetic activity can suppress. Deprived of his "business" and his faith in its importance, the retired citizen with no substitute activity sickens and dies. Even the typical active American must have recourse to periodic escape through alcohol, sex, bursts of prejudice or acts of violence, direct or sublimated, if he is to save himself from the neurosis or breakdown which more and more is becoming the hallmark of western "achievers."

The ecstatic, on the other hand, runs a different risk. The average man is so unused to the ecstatic's type of consciousness, and he is, perhaps unconsciously, so disturbed by the stirrings of his own mystic depths that he rejects the ecstatic as a "kook" or a madman. So society avoids the mystic who is forced to go his lonely way deprived of that wholesome social intercourse and ministry which is his destiny. We see this phenomenon in the biographies of artists like Van Gogh, and in the social and legal perils encountered by great prophets and leaders like Socrates, Jeremiah, Eckhart, Fox, and Jesus. As I have already indicated, we see it in our own day, when there is a tendency to cast all experimenters with the psychedelic drugs in the role of misguided youth or irresponsible fanatics.

Despite the derogation of the value of the psychedelics in psychotherapy by many psychiatrists, there is much sound evidence that remarkable cures have been effected through the agency of the drugs. There is also evidence that frequently dramatic personality change has occurred. Furthermore, the evidence suggests that these changes may be effected through the most pervasive and poignant urge of man, the hunger for a religious commitment to give meaning to life. By unlocking the doors to man's religious self and his closely associated esthetic self, the psychedelics simply serve as keys, or tools, to give a person access to his dormant potentialities. We hope that the key does not open a Pandora's box of furies. Occasionally, this happens, not only through these drugs, but through the agency of any ecstasy, artistic or religious.

We must not think that the psychedelics can be used without risk. I am thinking here, not so much of the risk of misunderstanding and alienation from one's friends, though this cannot be ignored, but the risk of prolonged psychotic episode, confusion, or even, though rarely, a permanent madness. The "bad trip" is a reminder of this danger. It also reminds us of the obvious fact that the drugs are no panacea in themselves. They are powerful tools which, in trained and experienced hands, may constitute a promising means of treating a variety of mental ills.

The psychedelics are far from effecting the invariable cure for mental illness that one might wish, and there is evidence that their special effectiveness is closely associated with their capacity to release ecstatic religious states. This may be the key to their proper use, and it may explain why certain investigators have concluded that LSD is so much more effective than others.

It also may explain why there is a consensus, though not unanimity, among psychedelic investigators that it is desirable for the investigating therapist to have had the psychedelic experience himself. Understanding the heightened consciousness so much better, he is both more tolerant of it, more intuitive in utilizing methods to bring it about and more willing to foster it through proper handling. This will also help to explain why investigators differ when they report the religious characteristics of subjects who have had the drugs administered to them. Leary and Savage, for example, have reported a higher percentage of subjects willing to describe their sessions as religious.[4]

For these reasons it seems strange that a prejudice exists in some quarters against allowing investigators to study the drugs if they have previously ingested psychedelic drugs themselves, on the ground that they cannot be impartial. Leaving aside the question as to just who, in this hotly controversial area, is actually impartial, one can raise the question whether depriving the investigator of experience is not tantamount to blinding him to the very area that will mediate therapeutic effects. It is significant that Czechoslovakia allows doctors to use the psychedelic drugs in experiments or practice *providing* they have had special training, including observation of at least thirty administrations and have taken the drugs at least five times themselves.[5] Indeed, some good LSD therapists have not taken the drug themselves. At the very least, however, the idea that the understanding of the procedure through previous practical experience might promote therapy should be considered a hypothesis to be investigated.

After these observations I will now present evidence that has persuaded me that religious experience is closely associated with the best therapeutic results.

LSD and Alcoholism. In 1953, when LSD was considered chiefly a psychotomimetic agent, Drs. A. Hoffer and H. Osmond, in a hotel room in Ottawa, discussed the possibility of artificially causing hopeless alcoholics to "hit bottom" by frightening them with the drug and so simulating in advance a theoretical attack of the D.T. horrors. In 1960, at a conference on the use of LSD, Dr. Hoffer reported on the results with sixty of these alcoholics for whom neither psychiatry, medicine, nor Alcoholics Anonymous had availed.[6] The subjects were given large doses with the result, surprising to the investigators, that many had ecstatic religious, rather than psychotomimetic, experiences. Even more surprising was the fact that, on a five-year follow-up, half were no longer drinking. Among this number, generally speaking, most had experienced religious ecstasy. Many who had not experienced it, had returned to drink.

In a book published much more recently, Hoffer and Osmond

confirmed such results in general, though they have identified a condition among some few alcoholics suggesting a contraindication for LSD. For this condition, which they have labelled *malvaria,* they report successful treatment with nicotinic acid.[7] They speak of the normal LSD dosage in their work as 200-300 mcgr., but they do not hesitate to administer very heavy doses of 500 mcgr., or more when they feel the occasion calls for it, particularly if such doses are necessary to release the transcendental experience.[8]

An interesting and more carefully controlled experiment to check on the Hoffer-Osmond results was carried out by P. O. O'Reilly in Moose Jaw, Saskatchewan.[9] Dr. O'Reilly was originally skeptical of the value of LSD in alcoholism, particularly because he thought there was excessive subjectivity in reports of its use. Sixty-eight patients seriously ill with alcoholism were selected for treatment. Only 6 percent had a history of uncontrolled drinking for less than six years, and all were considered chronic alcoholics. The subjects were used as their own controls, and their carefully assembled histories for a one-year period just previous to their treatment was compared with their responses evaluated in a follow-up from two to thirty-four months following. Each patient was evaluated for the two months immediately following, and this behavior was compared with behavior during the two months preceding the final evaluation date. Since no significant difference was found between these two evaluation periods, it was assumed that therapeutic results, or lack of them, were relatively permanent.

Each patient was admitted to the hospital and treated according to a standardized routine. Six days later they were given 200 mcgr. of LSD in a pleasant environment. The following day they were interviewed by a psychiatrist for abreactive purposes, and they were asked to write up their experience. They were discharged the next morning if their recovery was complete. Twenty-six patients, or 38 percent of the group were completely abstinent in the two months preceding the final follow-up. Others had improved, but they were classed with the nonabstainers. No factors outside the treatment process correlated with abstinence. Such variables as age, marital status, educational level, membership in AA or church groups, number of previous psychiatric treatments, years of uncontrolled drinking, the psychiatric diagnosis, all showed no significant relation to abstinence. Eight different psychiatrists administered the treatment, but none had significantly better results than any other. Only one factor was found to correlate significantly with abstinence at the .01 percent level of probability. This means that there was less than one chance in a hundred that, if the experience were repeated, a contrary finding would result. This correlating factor was that patients who experienced depression and/or claimed to have had a transcendental experience, without signs of physical distress or post-treatment disturbance, showed greater abstinence during follow-up. This criterion characterized 46 percent of abstainers and only 6 percent of the non-abstainers.

The project was noteworthy for at least three reasons. One often hears the criticism among scientists that enthusiasts report favorable results which others cannot obtain. The obvious retort is that experiments are often carried out by investigators firmly biased *against* the use of LSD. But this experiment was carried out by a skeptic who had never taken the drug himself. The second remarkable factor was that positive results were secured despite the fact that the treatment for these alcoholics was relatively so brief. Ordinarily no treatment was given after the one week—unless one might regard the two follow-up sessions as a form of treatment. The final noteworthy factor was that, like Hoffer and Osmond, O'Reilly reported that the change in drinking habits was associated with religious experience.

These two results may be contrasted with an even better controlled study reported by Dr. E. F. W. Baker of Toronto Western Hospital.[10] Two matched groups of ten chronic alcoholics each were selected at random. Under double blind conditions, one group was given 800 mcgr. of LSD and the other group a placebo in hospital surroundings but with the patients under restraint. Another group of ten taken from the normally treated population of the in-patient addiction research clinic of the hospital were used as additional controls. Several factors were studied, but no mention was made in the report of religious experience as a specific focus of the study. The thirty patients were followed up for one year and no significant difference in outcome of the three groups was discovered. In view of the importance of the religious factors in other studies, one must question whether this study did not leave out the crucial element. In other words, it may be not so much the LSD as the religious experience associated with it that helps the alcoholic to control his urges. Baker's study may be seen as strengthening my own contention.

Hoffer has summarized the results of the treatment of alcoholics with LSD reported by eleven investigators from 1953 to 1964. These 269 cases were followed up for periods ranging from two to thirty-six months. One hundred forty-five, or well over half of the total number of alcoholics were reported as much improved; forty-four improved, and eighty, or less than a third, no change. Of eighty comparison controls followed up from six to eighteen months afterward, eleven were much improved, seven improved, and sixty-two showed no change. In this summary Hoffer does not report the proportion of improved alcoholics who underwent transcendental experiences. However, most, if not all, of the investigators were alert to the importance of this element in effective treatment.[11]

It will be remembered that O'Reilly reported that successful therapy was associated, not only with the transcendental experience, but also with depression. Readers of William James as well as my own, *Psychology of Religion,* and other accounts will recall that normally experiences of conversion are preceded by painful experiences often described by evangelists as "conviction of sin."[12] Not enough information is given to enable us to clearly compare the two states, but one cannot avoid the speculation that there may be a connection.

This feature will also help to explain occasional suicides influenced by religious depression as well as some of the rare, but highly publicized, suicides touched off by LSD.[13] It would seem that this fact should not be considered a contraindication either for LSD therapy or religion, particularly when the depression itself would seem to be one of the agents making possible a new life. "Conviction of sin" leads to "surrender," a state of mind which causes a dramatically changed attitude, the "new life" or "rebirth." Collaterally, this reminds one of the advice usually given to the LSD subject not to resist unwelcome thoughts but to accept them and "flow with the stream."

One of the founders of Alcoholics Anonymous described to me the transcendental experience he credits with giving him control over his compulsive drinking. Years later he took LSD five or six times. This, he said, reinstated his original ecstasy, and consequently he wishes that LSD were more available to alcoholics. He would seem to support the position I have been taking.

As my manuscript goes to press, fresh confirmation has become available. Dr. W. N. Pahnke recently reported to the American Medical Association that but one treatment with LSD showed a significant improvement with 117 alcoholics, after six months, over controls, in global adjustment and drinking behavior. He stated, in effect, that the superiority over the controls was brought about by the "peak" or mystical experiences usually associated with high dosages. The study was done at Spring Grove State Hospital, Baltimore, Maryland.[11A]

LSD and the Criminal. The psychedelic drugs have demonstrated considerable promise in the area of help for the criminal. For a variety of reasons, criminals are most difficult to treat and to rehabilitate. At some prisons as many as 80 percent of those released can be expected back within a year. Many criminals, classed by psychologists as "psychopaths" or "sociopaths," seem to be incurably self-centered and chronically unable to fit into society. Intellectually they may be gifted people with ample intelligence to perceive the difference between right and wrong, but they have little or no capacity to *feel* effectively the difference in order to be guided by it. It is obvious that any tool or treatment to help us with these chronic misfits would be an unexpected blessing.

Yet the amount of experimentation in this area, though promising, has been very slight, and in quality it has not yet passed beyond the pilot stage of research. This neglect would be puzzling were one unacquainted with the violence of the prejudice against the psychedelics. Penal authorities, as public servants, are understandably hesitant to venture into a field likely to get them into political trouble. And yet there are ex-convicts free today that attribute their ability to stay out of jail to experiences sustained under psychedelic therapy. The bank robber whose case began this volume is one of them. Without his vision of Christ, he told me, his reform would have been impossible; without psilocybin, the vision would have been impossible.

One of the first reports to dent my own previous prejudice against the idea that drugs could trigger genuine and wholesome religious experience concerned work with convicts. The notion seemed preposterous, but I was influenced by Dr. Timothy Leary, at that time still in good graces but beginning to have differences of opinion with his colleagues at Harvard. After experiencing the power and some of the benefits of the psychedelic experience for myself, I was willing to consider a little more seriously the possibility that convicts could have such experiences, too.

According to one of Dr. Leary's superiors at Harvard, his research with the convicts was a shambles. Prison authorities, treatment staff and the convicts themselves were equally disillusioned, I was told. Since this information was so at variance with accounts given by Dr. Leary, it was obvious to me that, if I wished to appraise the situation, I would have to investigate for myself. Accordingly, I asked him to introduce me to some of the convicts who had been treated, and I visited the prison on that account.

On March 15, 1963, shortly after accounts of Dr. Leary's growing differences with Harvard authorities began to appear in the daily papers, I made my first visit. I had not been fifteen minutes behind the prison walls before it became evident that if anyone was disillusioned it was not the convicts. On one of the prisoners' bulletin boards was a picture of Dr. Leary cut from a newspaper and under it the following legend:

WARNING — DANGEROUS
WANTED   Timothy Leary, alias "Doc," alias "The Brain," age 40: height 6′ 1″: weight 190. Wears phony hearing aid; affects Harvard accent. Thought to have connections with Mafia International.

This man is dangerous. He is armed with compassion and the desire to help anyone in trouble.

Anyone who comes in contact with this desperado is asked to inform the State Police immediately.

Conversations with the members of the psilocybin project still in jail indicated that experiences under the drug had often been religious, the most clear-cut case being that of Mr. P., the armed robber before mentioned. He told me that, previous to his vision of Christ, he had never been troubled by a twinge of conscience and had volunteered solely for the purpose of combatting boredom and improving his chances for parole. This type of motivation was characteristic. Plans that Dr. Leary had made for the therapeutic follow-up of the thirty-six volunteers after their release collapsed following his troubles at Harvard. The recidivism rate in this group, compared to the general population at this prison, dropped sharply at first.[14] Five years later, the subjects still had a 23 percent advantage in improved recidivism over the general prison population even though they had received little attention from the original team of investigators.[15]

This improvement in the rate of recidivism was due in part to the formation of the Self-Development Group. Mr. P. and Mr. K., armed robbers serving long terms, and several members of the experimental group, organized the Self-Development Group to rehabilitate themselves and other convicts. With support from the State Commission on Correction, this organization has grown and spread to Deer Island House of Correction in Boston Harbor, a county jail. It now has an outside organization run by ex-convicts, but privately financed. By January, 1969, they had influenced the lives of some 300 convicts both in and out of prison. By lowering the recidivism rate the organization believes it has saved the taxpayers of Massachusetts from half a million to a million dollars. Even though the true figures should turn out to be only a tenth of this, this development, the chance fruit of an only partly executed drug experiment, ought to make criminologists think.

An interview with the late Mr. Edward S. Grennan, Superintendent of the Concord Reformatory, disclosed that, far from being disillusioned with Dr. Leary's project, he had been very much impressed with it and was anxious to have it followed up. He made the point, one on which all social scientists would agree, that the experiment would have been more convincing if a control group receiving equal attention but no drugs had been provided. As one critic put it, "Tim Leary alone could convert a stone!" Despite proposals of repetition with improved methodology, this promising pilot experiment has never been followed up, which reflects partly the difficult climate of opinion relating to the psychedelic drugs and partly the natural reluctance of official-dom to take risks.

However, there have been other tentative experiments along similar lines reported from abroad. One project was that of G. W. Arendsen-Hein, M.D., of Ederveen, Holland. He felt challenged to try the drug "in the so-called incurable and up to now hopeless cases . . . severe psychopathic personalities showing moral insanity, pseudologia phantastica, chronic alcohol-ism, sexual perversions, etc., who had long records of criminal behavior and at least five to twenty court sentences behind them."[16]

Twenty-one patients were treated in the open ward of a thera-peutic community, as far removed from a prison atmosphere as possible. They were told what to expect and at the same time a firm relationship among the patient, the therapist and a nurse was established, a process that took several weeks. They were then given doses of 50 to 450 mcgr. of LSD once every week or two weeks as the patient desired, over a period of ten to twenty weeks. Toward the end of each LSD session, patients were encouraged to express their experiences in free painting. This was followed by a group therapeutic discussion and a written personal report. This material was used in private conferences with the therapist and in further group sessions.

Among the valuable therapeutic effects of the drug was men-tioned "cosmic religious experiences" in some cases connected with liberation of "creative, auto-regulative and integrative powers of the ego," as well as great enrichment. The investigator also mentioned the fact that these corrective emotional expe-riences "may be even a restitution of faith in life, God and self," though he also mentioned the importance of putting these newly found values into practice, which was seen in the Leary experi-ment both in the practice and the breach. The period of follow-up is not mentioned, but during this time, of the twenty-one patients twelve were listed as clinically improved and two others much improved. Some had married and found better jobs with consequent emotional stabilization. "An inveterate swindler and sexual pervert, formerly judged morally insane and treated unsuccessfully during five previous years, is now such a different character that skeptics would say this is too good to be true."[17] If religious converts should volunteer similar descriptions—as has occurred in well authenticated cases[18]—the skeptics would still be ready to play their familiar role.

LSD and Terminal Illness. In *Island,* Aldous Huxley presents his dream of a utopian society in which the use of psychedelic drugs is built into the community at significant points in the life cycle, ending with preparation for death. Huxley acted out this aspect of the use of the "moksha medicine" in what has been reported as a particularly serene facing of death with the aid of LSD after he learned that he was ill with terminal cancer.

Probably the first systematic study of the usefulness of LSD in this capacity was at the University of Chicago Medical School by Dr. Eric Kast.[19] The subjects were 121 male and female hospital patients with terminal cancer whose death could be anticipated in one to two months. They were given 100 mcgr. of LSD and, when first symptoms appeared, they were simply told that they had received a potent medicine that might make them feel queer for awhile.

Among the results was not an abolition of the pain but a tolerance of it that appeared to be roughly ten times as effective as that produced by opiates. This was measured by the length of time that elapsed before the patient requested more relief.[20] Some relief from pain was noted for three weeks. Dr. Kast does not mention religious experience in his written account of the study, but he says that in general the patients were able to state that death was near and the situation hopeless but with acceptance. This, of course, suggests that to a considerable degree some form of religion was involved.

A more deliberate effort to utilize LSD's capacity for triggering religious experience to increase effectiveness in dealing with approaching death was reported by Walter N. Pahnke, M.D., in his Ingersoll Lecture at Harvard University in June, 1968.[21] At the Sinai Hospital in Baltimore, Maryland, a pilot program was carried out in which seventeen volunteers suffering from terminal cancer were given LSD one or more times. The subjects were told that the purpose of the drug was not to cure their physical illness but to help with their emotional adjustment along with the possibility of reducing their suffering. After screening and selection, three to ten hours were used in psychologically preparing the subject for treatment. Diagnosis of their disease was not mentioned unless the patient brought up the subject.

Of this group about one-third of the patients seemed not particularly helped, one-third helped somewhat, and one-third helped "dramatically." There were no indications of any harm, even with those who were physically very ill. Probably the most significant finding of the study was that the dramatic effects followed emergence of a "psychedelic mystical experience." Fear, anxiety and depression were lessened, and on this account sometimes the need for pain medication was also lessened. There was a striking increase in the ability to face the idea of death without fear, and from this Dr. Pahnke feels that most of the benefits flowed.

As an illustration of a representative result, though not completely mystical, he cites the case of a forty-nine-year-old grandmother with inoperable cancer of the pancreas. She was brought to the hospital by her husband and daughter after they could no longer tolerate at home her agony, and her increasing consequent mental deterioration, none of which could be controlled by con-

ventional medication and treatment. The family knew the diagnosis, but, as most families do, they kept it carefully concealed
from the patient. At his wit's end, the husband suggested "mercy
killing."

The LSD session was filled with religious symbolism, and with
moments when the patient strongly felt "the presence of God."[22]
There was a sense of release from certain guilt feelings, and at the
evening meeting with her family they noticed her increased relaxation and heightened mood. Her pain was now controllable by
narcotics. A few days later, she spontaneously asked the therapist
whether she had cancer. Her attending physician and the family
had previously advised that they disapproved telling her the
truth. However, she forced the issue, and in the resulting dramatic confrontation with the family it was the patient alone whose
inner strength reconciled her husband and daughter to an open
acceptance of her impending death. A second LSD session helped
her with the resolve to communicate appropriately with her
grandchildren about the situation. Following this, the patient
went home, and the family commented on how much better she
bore her pain in the month of life left to her. Death, which had
been a hidden chimera stalking the house, now became a spectre
whose terrors vanished when openly faced.

Dr. Pahnke comments on the benefits of the surrender to ego
loss in the transcendent mystical experience. In our highly individual and competitive society, great stress is placed on the
preservation of the ego, and one of the criticisms often heard
of the pyschedelic experience is that it may "abolish the ego"
when one gives over "control," another psychiatric shibboleth
in our scientific age. Indeed, it is this apprehension of approaching ego loss that often sends the LSD voyager into a panic and
constitutes a chief reason for the need of an experienced guide
to support endurance of the "ego death." Such an experience
constitutes the psychological foundation of the age old theme

of death and transfiguration celebrated by the ancients and the paradox that only he who has "died" can fully live. "Except a man be born again, he cannot see the kingdom of God,"[23] said Jesus to the bewildered Nicodemus. But for one who has undergone the psychedelic ego death, such statements lose their mystery. The courage to surrender one's self-hood, the "losing of one's life" that one may find it seems to be the key to that triumph over death of which our case has given us a fleeting glimpse. It helps us to understand what it means to face death with dignity. Too often our materialized medicine robs us of this right.

In view of such promise it is sad to learn that the American Cancer Society, despite knowledge of facts like these, has refused funds for following up such a promising means of alleviating the agony and dehumanization of the typical death by cancer, though they state that such a study should be made. On the other hand, such research underlines the role that religious experience, however brought about, may play in that mixture of high adventure and relaxed peace that constitutes the experience of dying for those who are properly prepared.

Grof's Research in Czechoslovakia. It is not possible to do justice to all the important contributions and brilliant research with LSD carried out in all parts of the globe, though principally in North America and Europe. Besides those whose names have already been mentioned above, there should be noted Hanscarl Leuner, M.D., of the University of Göttingen, Germany's leading expert on LSD therapy; Richard A. Sandison, D.P.M., of Powick Hospital in England, and H. A. Abramson, M.D., of the United States, who has not only carried on research, but has edited two important volumes containing contributions of experts in the field.[24]

Probably the most thorough, searching, and illuminating clinical account of research with LSD available in English comes from the pen of Stanislav Grof, M.D.[25] The bulk of his research was carried out in the Psychiatric Research Institute, Prague. The most interesting aspect of this work was his finding that most important for clinical effectiveness was the attainment of the mystical vision through "ego death." This, of course, confirms what other investigators have independently discovered about the importance of religious experience in effective psychotherapy with the psychedelic chemicals, and quite possibly without them as well.[26] However, it has never before been documented so clearly and effectively. This experimental group was made up of 50 hospitalized psychotics.

For our purposes, the most significant finding of the Grof study was that in so many of his subjects the pattern of improvement in symptomatology was similar. The most dramatic followed the experience of "ego death," reported as the melting away of the boundaries of the self. Apparently, this is identical with the achievement of unity characteristic of the mystical consciousness. The ego death, properly guided and supported by the therapist, would be followed by the sense of rebirth, the "putting on of the new man," "redemption," or "salvation" spoken of in scriptural passages; or the achieving of "illumination," "ekatvam," "nirvana," "sartori," or whatever the term used in some of the non-Christian traditions. The course of therapy following successive doses of LSD for three classes of subjects—psychotics, neurotics, and normals—is schematically shown in the accompanying figure. This represents a general summary of clinical impressions.

Of interest to psychotherapists is the fact that therapy at succeeding stages supports the insights of Freud, Rank and Jung. Seemingly, successive layers of the unconscious are exposed. First, the visionary material of the sessions disclose the Freudian personal unconscious of the subject with its childhood trauma and Oedipal material. Then comes the stressful ego death through the birth trauma emphasized by Rank, followed by the experience of rebirth, and, at longer or shorter intervals, a dramatic improvement of symptoms. Following the rebirth, Jungian symbolism is seen to dominate the visionary experience with religious archetypes and the spontaneous use of religious terminology as subjects struggle to describe what has happened to them.

As others have done, Grof distinguishes between a series of lower dosage LSD sessions (50-400 mcgr.), called "psycholytic therapy," prevalent in Europe as typified in the methods developed by Leuner in Germany, and the "psychedelic" method which aims to achieve the ego death in one large dose (250-1,500 mcgr.). In either case, Grof feels that the goal should be the ego death, and treatment should not be considered successful until this has been achieved. In this sense, both methods may be extremes of the same continuum. He also points out that growth toward psychological and spiritual health continues beyond the treatment period.

Healthy subjects attain the ego death much more rapidly than the sick. The length of treatment is roughly proportional to the severity of the illness. The rather amazing (to psychotherapists) results are that *all* groups finally achieved, not just average, but superior adjustment. This seems to support not only the claims of Jung that all problems tend ultimately to be religious, but also the assertions of A. H. Maslow regarding "self-actualization."

Through experience and trial and error, Grof has discovered that certain types of patients, notably severe obsessive-compulsives, seldom achieve ego death, so LSD therapy for them seems contraindicated; and to a lesser degree the same may be true of certain hysterics. Consequently the schema presented must not be generalized to all types of the mentally ill. The curves pre-

Representing Clinical Condition of Subjects
in Free Intervals Between Sessions in Successful Psycholytic Treatment with LSD.[27]

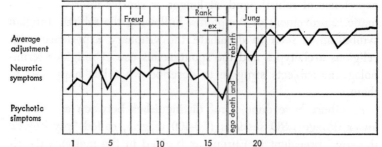

Neurotic patients:

Average
adjustment

Neurotic
symptoms

Psychotic
simptoms

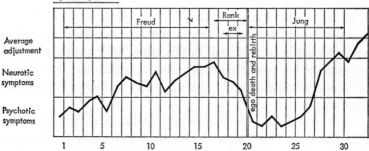

Psychotic patients:

Average
adjustment

Neurotic
symptoms

Psychotic
symptoms

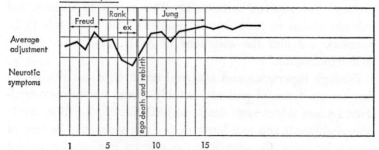

Normal subjects:

Average
adjustment

Neurotic
symptoms

Vertical Axis: clinical condition

Horizontal Axis: number of LSD sessions

sented represent a certain amount of selection in that types unlikely to profit were more and more often excluded as experience accumulated. Nevertheless, the results suggest that many of the mentally ill now held in hospitals could be released through properly applied LSD treatment. Even normals may improve their functioning. A key feature is the religious element. Surely these results call for careful and critical testing by psychotherapists and religious scholars alike.

Summary. This chapter started with a discussion, through allusions to both ancient and modern examples, of the power of religion to change personality and individual lives at a profound level, though these changes may be accompanied by certain risks. Because of its capacity to trigger very similar, if not identical, states, LSD-type chemicals enable us to mobilize and study such changes so that we can utilize them in correcting certain abnormal conditions and making individual lives richer, more fulfilling and more effective.

The pioneer research of Hoffer and Osmond with alcoholics showed that one large dose of LSD, when the result was transcendental or "psychedelic," was effective in maintaining abstinence. Without this experience, treatment was no better that other methods.

Other studies seem to support this conclusion. Indications are that the effective agent is the religious experience however it may come about. The drugs simply serve as tools, or one means of triggering the experience, though a very effective means. Though studies with criminal psychopaths have been slighter, there is good reason for believing that the same thing is true in this area. There was a brief review of the value of LSD in alleviating the pain of terminal cancer and the stimulation among many patients of dramatically improved attitudes toward death.

Finally, the large amount of research with LSD in the field

of mental illness was represented by allusions to the studies of Grof in Czechoslovakia. His research offers dramatic opportunities to study the structure of man's unconscious with particular support at different levels for the theories of Freud, Rank, and Jung. What makes Grof's research so appropriate to the chapter is the fact that he has identified the experience of ego loss, with consequent psychological "death and rebirth" experience, the crucial episode and aim of therapy with LSD. This experience seems to parallel classical religious experience of a profound variety. It is significant that not only can certain psychotics be brought to normality, but that psychotics, neurotics and normals can be introduced to a level of superior functioning previously unknown to them. Such results require critical but open-minded and vigorous investigation, because of their practical value in psychotherapy and their contribution to personality theory.

NOTES

1. John Henry Newman, quoted in article by John Coulson, *Commonweal* (June 15, 1962).
2. Ruth Fox, M.D., in H. A. Abramson, ed., *The Use of LSD in Psychotherapy and Alcoholism* (Indianapolis: Bobbs-Merrill, 1967), p. 480.
3. Irving Stone, *Lust for Life: The Story of Vincent Van Gogh* (New York: Pocket Books, Inc., 1945), or other biographies.
4. R. E. L. Masters and J. Houston, *The Varieties of Psychedelic Experience* (New York: Holt, Rinehart and Winston, 1966), p. 254 ff.
5. Information obtained from Stanislav Grof, M.D., of the Psychiatric Research Institute, Prague, and Johns Hopkins University.
6. H. A. Abramson, ed., *The Use of LSD in Psychotherapy* (New York: Josiah Macy, Jr. Foundation, 1960), pp. 18-19, 114-15.
7. A. Hoffer and H. Osmond, *New Hope for Alcoholics* (New Hyde Park, N.Y.: University Books, 1968).
8. *Ibid.*, p. 92.
9. H. A. Abramson, ed., *The Use of LSD in Psychotherapy and Alcoholism* (Indianapolis: Bobbs-Merrill, 1967), pp. 504-510.

10. *Ibid.*, especially pp. 199-200. A full report will be found in R. G. Smart, T. Storm, E. F. W. Baker and L. Solursh, *Lysergic Acid Diethylamide (LSD) in the Treatment of Alcoholism* (Toronto: University of Toronto Press, 1967).

11. Abramson, *Use of LSD*, p. 351.

11A. Reported to the 118th. Annual Meeting of the American Medical Association, New York City, July 17, 1969, at Symposium on Psychedelic Drugs.

12. W. James, *Varieties*, lectures 8-10; W. H. Clark, *The Psychology of Religion* (New York: Macmillan, 1958), Chap. 9.

13. S. Cohen's extensive survey reported no suicides among several thousand normal volunteers taking LSD and only 4 among a similar number of patients. S. Cohen, "LSD Side Effects and Complications" *Journal of Nervous and Mental Disease* (1960), pp. 130-140.

14. T. Leary and W. H. Clark, "Religious Implications of Consciousness Expanding Drugs," *Religious Education,* 58 (May-June, 1963), pp. 251-256; T. Leary, *High Priest* (New York: World Publishing Co., 1968), pp. 173-211. For a report of his experiences by one of the convicts, see G. Castayne, "The Crime Game" in R. Metzner, ed., *The Ecstatic Adventure* (New York: Macmillan, 1968).

15. Information received from Dr. Ralph Metzner, one of Dr. Leary's associates in this work.

16. Reported in R. Crockett, et al., eds., *Hallucinogenic Drugs and their Psychotherapeutic Use* (Springfield, Ill.: C. C. Thomas, 1963), pp. 101-106. Dr. Arendsen-Hein has also referred in part to the same project in a discussion in which he goes more deeply into religious aspects of the drug experience in Abramson, *Use of LSD,* pp. 569-576. Also personal communication.

17. Crockett, *op. cit.*

18. W. James, *Varieties*; W. H. Clark, *The Oxford Group* (New York: Bookman Associates, 1951); H. Begbie, *Twice Born Men* (New York: Fleming H. Revell Co., 1909).

19. E. Kast, "Pain and LSD-25" in D. Solomon, ed., *LSD: The Consciousness-Expanding Drug* (New York: G. P. Putnam's Sons, 1964).

20. Stated by Dr. Kast in a lecture at Massachusetts Institute of Technology before the Neurobiological and Psychedelic Study Group, 1964.

21. *Harvard Theological Review,* 62, 1 (January, 1969). Some of the material in my report derived from personal conversation following the lecture.

22. *Ibid.*

23. Jn. 3:3.

24. Leuner's compendious volume *Die Experimentelle Psychose: Ihre Psychopharmakologie, Phänomenologie und Dynamik in Beziehung zur Person* (Berlin: Springer-Verlag, 1962) has not been translated into English. Sandison assisted R. Crockett to edit *Hallucinogenic Drugs and their Psychotherapeutic Use* (Springfield, Ill.: Chas. C. Thomas, 1963). Abramson's two volumes are *The Use of LSD in Psychotherapy* (New York: Josiah Macy Foundation, 1960) and *The Use of LSD in Psychotherapy and Alcoholism* (Indianapolis: Bobbs-Merrill, 1967).

25. A summary of Dr. Grof's work is available in the 1967 Abramson volume cited in Note 20 above, pp. 154-190, though without references to Freud, Rank and Jung hereafter to be cited. The latter information was derived from lectures by Dr. Grof at the Massachusetts Institute of Technology sponsored by the Neurobiological and Psychedelic Study Group and personal conversation, but chiefly from Dr. Grof's brilliant manuscript volume, doubtless destined to be an important contribution when published, *Theory and Practice of LSD Psychotherapy*.

Dr. Grof with Z. Dytryck has published in Czech the two-volume *LSD-25 and Its Use in Clinical Practice,* partly available in a German translation. At present writing Dr. Grof is in the United States doing work at Johns Hopkins University and Spring Grove State Hospital Research Center, Baltimore, Md.

26. Compare with the importance of the religious experience in the treatment of alcoholism reported by the Salvation Army and Alcoholics Anonymous, the emphasis on religion in Jungian therapy, not to speak of the access of effective personal power in saints and religious leaders after religious experience, Moses, Socrates and St. Teresa of Avila.

27. Stanislav Grof, M.D., Table "Representing Clinical Condition of Subjects in Free Intervals Between Sessions in Successful Psycholytic Treatment with LSD." Used with permission of author.

8. Drugs and Responsible Religion

And this is that wayless being which all interior spirits have chosen above all other things. This is the dark silence in which all lovers lose themselves. But if we would prepare ourselves for it by means of the virtues, we should strip ourselves of all but our very bodies, and should flee forth into the wild Sea, whence no created thing can draw us back again.

—Jan van Ruysbroeck[1]

By their fruits ye shall know them. —Jesus of Nazareth[2]

I will now return to some of the issues raised in the opening chapter and in the discussion on "Religion and Ecstasy." The point was made that at least three important trends in recent western expression of religion need to be understood and coordinated. First, the characteristic western emphasis on rationality expresses itself in an increased interest in theology and in efforts to coordinate religious concepts with scientific findings. Second, there are the efforts to "secularize" religion, the "death of God" movement and the insistence that religion identify itself with the life of the marketplace, the world of politics, the cause of human rights and alleviation of human suffering. Finally, there is the return to the interior life which, in many forms, shows itself both within and outside institutionalized religion.

It is within this last trend that the religious expressions of the users of the psychedelics belong. Their natural parallels are Zen Buddhism and "speaking in tongues." In more traditional

117

forms, emphasis on the "Inner Light" of the Friends and on mysticism in Swedenborgianism is still very strong, while the Hasidic tradition among the Jews seems to be undergoing a modest revival. In Roman Catholicism the contemplative life has never entirely disappeared; its mystical strain has been an important source of spiritual strength without which the amazing durability of the church would have been impossible. Contemplative orders, like the Cistercians, have been agents of the preservation of these values. The life of the late Thomas Merton and the popular acceptance of his writings is an indication of a modern interest in mysticism among Catholics that may become a seed for wider growth.

Zen has not been the only influence from the East. The late saintly Swami Akhilananda was beloved by many Christians, while the Vedanta movement in America that he represented has become influential in many Ashrams. A succession of religious visitors to the West from the East, and particularly from India, have had influence on different individuals varying from exceedingly superficial to very profound.

It follows that what I will have to say about chemically induced states and responsible religion will refer in some measure to all of these movements, partly as a foil and means of comparison, partly as an occasion for raising certain issues and pointing out dilemmas which religion must face.

The Problem of Communicating Ecstasy. Mysticism and religious ecstasy involve most basically a subjective perception of exceeding clarity and vividness. Sometimes the accompanying visions carry a meaning which can be described in terms that make sense to others, but more often it seems impossible to describe the subjective enlightenment. The prophet and the mystic are apt to be thought fuzzy minded, if not feeble minded or mad. Even the mystic himself may doubt the significance of his own vision and discard it when he finds that he has difficulty in conceptualizing it. He is forced to speak in riddles even to himself, and he must become a poet to speak at all. Asked to describe God, instead of rattling off a list of attributes, like a theologian, he may speak of "the dark silence in which all lovers lose themselves."

The mystic comes to feel that he lives in two worlds, the world of sense and values, which he shares with all humankind, and the world of his vision, which has startled him with its strangeness. It makes nonsense of his previously held values and can be fully shared only with other mystics. He asks himself which is true, the objective world he can so neatly and clearly describe, which others so readily comprehend, or that subjective, inner world which captivates his inner sense and promises to make him a new man. To follow the inner world will lead him far from the familiar haunts of sense and his fellow men. Indeed, he may find that to be obedient to his "heavenly vision" he is called on to leave father and mother, wife and children and "flee forth into the wild Sea, whence no created thing" can draw him back again.

This is the kind of dilemma which ingesters of LSD often face, which helps to explain why the "unilluminated" find it so dangerous. An example which suggests real physical danger will be found in the last chapter of Timothy Leary's *High Priest*, when the urge to drive off a cliff during a wild auto ride seemed so attractive. But the dilemma is ages old, and, in different form, is essentially symbolized in the Allegory of the Cave found in Plato's *Republic*.

The Issue of Quietism. A related problem is that of whether one should consider the ecstatic vision, the encounter with God, as an end in itself or as a means to a life of righteousness and good works. The problem is somewhat similar to the argument over "art for art's sake." The problem is ancient and has been argued with differing emphases in the West and East alike. In general, western faiths have deplored and sometimes savagely condemned what in seventeenth century Catholic tradition was labeled the heresy of Quietism. But the defeat of the mystics Molinos, Fenelon and Madame Guyon has not settled the issue. Their writings still attract both Catholic and non-Catholic readers. Doubtless, their anti ecclesiasticism had much to do with their condemnation.

Nevertheless, few of even the most devoted contemplatives have written of the Beatific Vision as if it were completely severed from a life of love and charity. "Charisma" generated a following, as with St. Francis, through lives filled with the fruits of compassionate natures. St. Anthony, one of the most austere of the mystics, spent many solitary years devoted to meditation. But when the political situation needed him, he emerged to serve his fellow men. When affairs grew calmer, he returned to his meditation.[3]

The Roman Catholic Church has required, as one of the criteria for sainthood, conformity with Christian teaching in act as well as word. Even the Christian mystics who have been declared heretical, like the great scholastic, Meister Eckhart, exalted acts of mercy over selfish enjoyment of the presence of God. He wrote:

If a man was in rapture such as St. Paul experienced, and if he knew a person who needed something of him, I think it would be far better out of love to leave the rapture and serve the needy man.[4]

The Buddha himself eschewed Nirvana until, through his efforts, all mankind could be illumined.

We do live in two worlds, one of practical living, the other metaphysical, which the ordinary religious believer calls "the world of the spirit," whose source is symbolized by the name of God. One cannot live very long in the practical world of sense, especially beset with difficulty and tragedy, without asking about the meaning of existence. Furthermore, one's hold on life will not remain durable without some reference to the metaphysical, that mystery which will explain this strange journey from birth to death. The best demonstration to the practical man that "there may be some good in religion" is an intense direct experience of "God," "Nirvana," or "Ultimate Reality," which reassures him that life, after all, *is* worth living. Several persons I have known have been saved—some by psychedelics—from suicide through religious experience that surprised them with a sense of a meaning of life far beyond what they had previously known.

This means that the religious man, this citizen of two worlds, must somehow find a way of balancing one against the other. One world dictates the imperative of taking care of bodily survival and related affairs, rational and critical explanations, religious institutions and "good works." The other grants the inner world of vision. Balance between the practical and the experience of the Ultimate has been the aim of monastic and utopian communities in many cultures. The "hippie" communities that have grown up recently, many of which have at least owed their inception to use of the psychedelics, can be looked on as a monastic movement of the present day. Some are admirable social experiments; others shabby and irresponsible. Most are a mixture of the two; few have had a long enough history to judge accurately.[5]

Many responsible people are alarmed by the hippies' advocacy of "dropping out." In practice, this has a variety of meanings. "Dropping out" may mean anything from a sane and wholesome taking of moral stock as a means of spiritual renewal, to a complete abdication of responsibility and effort. The concept of the Sabbath, at least theoretically, is simply a weekly "dropping out" from everyday activity for the purpose of reflection and spiritual renewal. Plato prescribed a similar periodic rest from the affairs of state for the Guardians in *The Republic* that they might refresh themselves with the "dear delight of philosophy." A modern commentator, Eric Erikson, speaks of the desirability of a "psycho-social moratorium" for a youth if he is to cope successfully with his "identity crisis," to discover himself and become a man.

Many a hippie, or part-time hippie, has put his sojourn in a community of "drop-outs" to good use. There is no universally applicable principle to determine who will and who will not profit from such an experience. If one is to escape the charge of quietism, sooner or later he will be required to justify his withdrawal, both to himself and to the society of which he is a part. I simply wish to present two sides and to point out that at the very least there is a danger of irresponsible withdrawal and escape of which everyone who tries the drugs should be aware.

Part of the problem comes from the popular misunderstanding of "instant mysticism." A residual Calvinism frowns on anything easy. Those who would never think of undergoing the ordeal idealize a twenty-year sojourn in a monastery or some similar labor as the only proper road to true enlightenment. Such people forget the central theological concept of grace. But it will be very real to any conscientious religious person who has undergone the awesome and amazing experience of the ingestion of LSD. Some of God's gifts come unbidden and undeserved, for example, the appearance of Christ to St. Paul on the Damascus road, or to Mr. P., the convict, whom I have mentioned before. The hard work comes after the gift has been recognized and accepted. Some of these issues are discussed by Rabbi Zalman Schachter in his reflections on his experience under LSD in Metzner's, *The Ecstatic Adventure.*

The emphasis on activism and good works in western faiths provides a wholesome check on the extreme subjectivism and neglect of social justice in some expressions of eastern religion. Eckhart's statement that the mystic should leave his vision of God if his neighbor had any need of him is a case in point. In addition, one may question whether it is good for the westerner to desert completely that tradition in which he has his roots. Although this may sometimes be desirable, one may find warnings in many an inappropriate conversion. It is not hard to graft the type of experience triggered by the psychedelics onto the Quaker faith, the great mystical tradition of Roman Catholicism, Jewish Hasidism or Muslim Sufism. There is required first an open-minded but critical study of the facts, then the courage to experiment.

The counterargument, of course, is that the busy man of affairs ordinarily has no time for this laborious spiritual adventure. The quicker path may not be the same, but it may accomplish its end if it makes one more sensitive, is followed up by disciplined attention to the insights attained and ushers the individual into a wider, more effective life of spiritual commitment. Whether this is the case with any considerable numbers of the drug takers can be determined not by *a priori* assumptions, but by careful following up the actual results and the conditions determining responsible religious use of the chemicals. As I have pointed out, this seems to be the case with respect to the Native American Church. Perhaps here is a case where the exploited Indian may return good for evil by providing instruction and example for modern America.

The Issue of Institutionalization. One of the characteristics of ecstatic religion is that the mystic or ecstatic must be free and open to that uprushing influence that fills him with a sense of mystery and awe, even though he may feel threatened by it. This is why the good guide in a psychedelic session will both support the subject and encourage him to forget his defenses, to relax and let the experience take him where it will. This function requires considerable experience and even courage on the part of the guide himself. This openness to the *mysterium tremendum* begets a sense of freedom that carries over into other spheres of religion. Consequently, mystics as a group have never been noted for their docility to ecclesiastical discipline. But whether their aim is to be associated with other mystics or to multiply their influence through some form of transcendental community, there developed the need for mutual cooperation, which is the beginning of most of the established faiths and churches. Even the Twelve appointed a treasurer.

But there are other cogent reasons for directing the energies of ecstasy. I have spoken of the need for balance between the rational and nonrational functions of the religious consciousness if any religious venture is to be successful. An appropriate institution may, through its teachings, guide the impulses awakened by ecstasy into creative channels. On the other hand, ecstasy, too often repeated, may degenerate into an unprofitable orgy of sensation.

One may raise the question whether the ecstasy released by the drugs *can* be institutionalized. The answer is very simply given. It has been. For this is the case with the use of peyote by the Indians of the Native American Church mentioned above. True the institutionalization is very loose, but the ceremonies surrounding the sacramental consumption of peyote are well structured, as is the behavior of adherents who are taught the duties of hard work, family responsibility and abstinence from alcohol. Thus the church supplies an ethical framework which enlists the nonrational energies released by the sacrament to combat the besetting weaknesses of its members. If other similar churches are formed, a parallel framework should be supplied. To the objection that any psychedelic will soon become institutionalized, and that therefore a new road to ecstasy will need to be found, as Dr. Leary believes,[6] we may reply that the means to nonrational experience is almost built into a "psychedelic" church.

If the drugs are to be used at all in any institution, they must be used sparingly, as they are in the Native American Church. Any religious organization using them must remember that there are other roads to spirituality, even if it should turn out that the drugs are the *best* road for some. All we can be sure of at the moment is that *for some people* in certain circumstances the drugs may perform an important function. An organization to take the responsibility of ordaining skilled, competent and dedicated ministers to administer the psychedelic sacrament may perform a function that no other type of organization can. At the same time it would enable members to exercise their constitutional right to use these chemicals religiously. However, it should provide the safeguards that the public has every right to expect against their socially harmful use.

Those whose information about the drugs comes chiefly from the fevered accounts in the news media or the warnings of ill-informed psychiatrists may fear that a church dispensing psychedelic drugs could only create wholesale addiction. We can refer to the Native American Church in support of the conviction that this will not take place. (Again I must repeat, there is little evidence that the psychedelics *are* addicting.) Usually the drugs, used religiously, are simply the means of making people aware of their religious potentialities, thereby linking them consciously with a great tradition of prophets, saints and martyrs. In this way they find meaning in what they had thought were merely the empty pious phrases of the churches.

With this breakthrough behind them, the probabilities are that drugs will play a progressively less central place in their religious practices.[7] This has been the tendency among many of Dr. Leary's former associates, such as Dr. Richard Alpert.

It is not true that these persons regret their use of the drugs in the first place. Formally or informally, I have followed up approximately 300 users of the psychedelics. Of these well over half have felt the main impact of the drugs to have been religious. None, when closely questioned, have not reported at least some elements of profound religious experience. So far I have yet to find even one who is unequivocally sorry he took the drugs, though a number have given them up.[8] This tendency has also characterized many of the more responsible utopian communities where the drugs formerly had more importance, such as the United Illuminators, a very creative community with their center at Fort Avenue Terrace in the Roxbury section of Boston, publishers of *American Avatar*. Their publication—to be distinguished from *Avatar*, from which it has separated itself—is one measure of the quality of this community.

The Springs of Religion. A sports promoter who neglected the springs of sport in the natural delight of rivalry in skillfully coordinated and harmonious bodily movement would be unlikely to build a durable sports empire. Similarly, the university which neglects the springs of learning in that joyful interplay of luminous minds and delight in acquiring wisdom is threatened with mediocrity and by student revolt. "Let me make the songs of the Nation," said Robert Burns, "and I care not who makes its laws!" The great nation has as much need for poetry and passion as it has for its legal code.

In like manner, the church that neglects the springs of religion in the nonrational functions of the human unconscious reaps the fruits of this neglect in progressive ossification. Church structures and missions become bland and harmless, or demonic in their thirst for power. A responsible religion concerns itself with some form of ecstatic renewal, remembering the part that passion born of ecstasy has played in the early stages of most religious movements.

The use of LSD, particularly in a religious environment with a competent guide, is a ready way of stirring deeply buried sources of the religious life and perceptions, which create feelings of awe, joy, wonder, peace and love. Sometimes, too, there appear the specters of terror, self-judgment, hellish tortures, distortions, insanity and death, so that one requires a stout heart and a steady guide if one is to emerge spiritually toughened rather than bruised from his "trip." In his passage he discovers his kinship with the poet, the musician and the artist and perhaps with some of the great intellectual voyagers who have been mystics as well as scientists and philosophers. It is such passionate pilgrims who have made religion go, without whom religion would long since have completely lapsed into that dessicated and bland affair that it has already become for so many respectable churchgoers.

The very depth of the roots of the religious life in the unconscious frightens many, and it is at least one reason why the use of the psychedelic drugs causes hysterical fear. With intrepid courage man explores the ocean's depth, climbs dizzying and snow-covered peaks, penetrates the darkness of the Arctic or ventures into the vastnesses of space. For this he gains almost unanimous applause. When he peers into *inner* space, he is likely to draw back in terror; and unless he does retreat, his companions brand him foolhardy or ridicule him for "contemplating his navel." St. Augustine said long ago:

And men go forth to wonder at the height of mountains, the huge waves of the sea, the broad flow of the rivers, the extent of the ocean, and the courses of the stars, and omit to wonder at themselves . . .[9]

A responsible religion dare not neglect this source of wonder, for it is in this way that God is perceived.

It is the terror, the joy and the risks of the religious life that are in some way inseparable from its effectiveness. Man approaches those most intimate concerns buried deeply within himself with dread, although he faces almost any danger that is open and plain to see with intrepid courage. It is not so much the statistical chance of things going wrong in the use of the psychedelics that produces the witch hunt, the hue and cry against those who misuse them. It is the fear of the unknown, of the "forms that swim and the shapes that creep under the waters of sleep" that so terrorize the ordinary man, both educated and uneducated.

This does not mean that there are not true risks, but that one must properly calculate them, then have the courage to act on the calculation. This has always been a large element in the progress of science, and it is always present in some form when high religion is involved, whether this religion is to be approached through the psychedelic drugs or in some other way.[10] It is the only kind of religion for which brave men have any respect, and it is the only kind that works. A great deal of society's refusal to grant sufficient freedom for experimenting properly with the psychedelics can be blamed, not so much on knowledgeable caution relative to their dangers, as to this failure of nerve in the face of the unknown.

The ancients knew that risks were involved in ecstatic religious experience; yet they discovered how often he who faced such fearsome adventures was rewarded by escaping the dangers and becoming a "new man." Likewise, the persistent inquirer into the psychedelic drugs is amazed, not that these powerful chemicals should be so dangerous, but that they should be relatively so safe.[11] These phenomena can be compared with the insights of many of the ancients who have described "trips" to the underworld and to hell—though it should be noted, always with a competent guide and with courage—from which the voyager almost always returned wiser and unscathed.

Just why such an ordeal should be so safe is an issue that will not be settled until science has probed considerably further into the mysteries of mind. All we have to rely on are intuitions and guesses, and here the best speculations available to us come from the people who have subjected themselves to the influence of the psychedelics and have conceived theories, no matter how fanciful, which appeal to them as explanations of such strange internal adventures. The leading theorist remains Dr. Timothy Leary who, no matter what has been implied to the contrary, is a brilliant scientific theorist as well as a poet and a mystic. Furthermore, unlike most of his critics, but like William James, he has actually "been there." He believes that the long history of the human race has built into our genes through DNA and RNA the accumulated wisdom that enables man to "trust his cells," which will bring him home to a safe haven despite the intensity of the ecstasy whether of heaven or of hell. The "ego death" is followed by rebirth.[12]

The cry from the scientific critics of the psychedelic drugs is that we don't know how they work, the implication being that they should not be used until we understand everything about them. We never may know all about them, any more than we will know how the English roast beef and humble garden vegetables eaten by Shakespeare turned into *Hamlet* or how the dull earthworm is transmuted into the song of the bird. Doubtless his friends worried about the playwright when they observed the poet with his eyes "in a fine frenzy rolling." But certain things that humankind has come to value—and, indeed, those things that we value most—cannot be had apart from ecstasy. Fortunately, Socrates, Moses, Gautama, St. Francis, St. Paul and Jesus did not have a representative of the American Medical Association at their elbows when the spirit came. Perhaps the time may come when we will feel the same way about Timothy Leary.

However, we should carefully observe those who ingest the drugs, with religious purpose or otherwise, provided only that we are open minded as well as critical. If organized religion is not sure enough of itself to face the religious issues posed by the drugs, then it deserves the contempt with which many of the most idealistic of the rising generation regard it. In such matters any responsible religious institution must keep alert to well-attested reports of damage, physical or psychological, done by the drugs, and they must put this information in the debit column as to their religious use and weigh the risk.

This is simply to say that churches, as well as psychiatrists, must be pragmatic. But the values, standards and methods of religious people will always differ to some degree from those of psychiatrists. Religion that has sold out to psychiatry is no longer religion. Yet both reject minute mechanical explanations and follow the general rule, "By their fruits ye shall know them." Certainly psychiatry and religion may approach one another. Their kinship is clearest in those areas where we have shown that profound religious experience often is followed by the best therapeutic results judged by the criteria accepted in psychiatry. The part that LSD has played in this demonstration has been documented in the previous chapter.

Dangers of LSD-type Drugs. As I have already indicated, any responsible religious use of the psychedelics will involve a frank facing of their dangers. The most comprehensive study of undesirable side effects of the drugs that I know about was published in 1960 by Dr. Sidney Cohen.[13] Forty-four experimenters with LSD gave 25,000 doses of the drug to 5,000 individuals, both normal volunteers and psychiatric patients. There were no suicides among the normals, and fewer than one administration in a thousand resulted in psychotic reactions lasting longer than forty-eight hours. One ingestion out of 2,500 involved suicide attributable in some degree to LSD. However, these figures were reported by experimenters who had experience in the use of the

drugs. Although we have no exact figures, irresponsible administration of the drugs will surely cause more frequent side effects.

Another charge made against LSD is that it causes brain
damage and "reduces people to vegetables." There is no evidence
that the LSD-type drugs, in dosages normally given, have any
such result. A research neurosurgeon told me that he had given
to animals fifty to a hundred times the maximum dosages taken
by humans, but autopsies showed no observable nerve damage.[14]

There is somewhat more evidence that these drugs may have
deleterious effects on chromosomes, and, under certain conditions,
might possibly cause genetic damage. Even this evidence is
sketchy and controversial. If LSD is to be suspected, so should
caffeine and other commonly used drugs. When such results are
positive, they are usually derived from experiments in animals
where dosages are very much higher than in humans. The only
properly controlled chromosomal study to come to my attention
to date involved 32 patients given pure LSD at Spring Grove
State Hospital, Baltimore, Maryland, with chromosomal assays
preformed both immediately before and immediately after dosage
by LSD. No significant difference in chomosomal breakages was
noted.[14A]

However, these experiments suggest that pregnant women, to
be on the safe side, would be well advised to omit all but medically
prescribed drugs, particularly in the early months. In this field, as
in any other, such as fasting, prolonged meditation or other artificial means of producing ecstasy, a responsible faith will keep
up-to-date on all the effects in that awesome and complicated
field we call religion.[15]

Summary. The type of experience stimulated by the psychedelics
is characterized by nonrational stirrings of the inner life, the root
of religion. The man of faith is faced with the dilemma as to
whether the inner or outer life is the truer reality, and so his

religion is threatened by quietism. Responsible religion will always use the test of results to counter the danger of quietism.

Although psychedelic communities seldom last long, they do serve some youth well as a retreat for meditating on their own problems as well as the problems of society. Use of the drugs as a road to "instant mysticism" also has some advantages over the more laborious ways to arrive at mysticism. Drug-induced mysticism is an expression of grace in modern form. Its undoubted depth and vitality provides a wholesome corrective to the highly structured and rationalized religious organizations. Each needs the other. LSD introduces many people to a vital religious life. However, it yields diminishing returns over the longer term unless it is used sparingly.

Responsible religion cannot neglect these demands of the inner life or avoid the dilemmas posed. Yet man's fear of his personal "unknown" in his unconscious, which has persisted through the ages, seems one of the powerful sources of social repression of the psychedelics, both by medicine and religion. When one is acquainted with its power, he is not surprised that psychedelic experience is so dangerous, but that it is so relatively safe. The fact that it is not always safe requires the voyager to take a calculated risk. Besides the psychological hazards of the drugs there are also possibilities of physical harm which cannot be neglected. But sober consideration of such studies as we have indicates that these certainly have been greatly exaggerated. And it must be remembered that, whether they have worked out the matter consciously or not, and whatever its source and nature, great religious figures have never been afraid of risk.

NOTES

1. Jan van Ruysbroeck in W. T. Stace, ed., *The Teachings of the Mystics* (New York: New American Library, 1960), p. 169.

2. Matt. 7:16.
3. For a semipopular and sensitive account of St. Anthony, see R. Fülöp-Miller, *The Saints That Moved the World* (New York: Collier Books, 1962).
4. Quoted in W. T. Stace, *Teachings of the Mystics,* p. 338.
5. See R. Houriet, "Life and Death of a Commune called Oz," *New York Times Magazine* (Feb. 16, 1969).
6. T. Leary, *High Priest,* p. 323.
7. Dr. William H. McGlothlin of the University of California, Los Angeles, is engaged in a study of former LSD users. In informal conversation he has spoken of the same trend, though his research has not been concluded.
8. This statement is supported through verbal inquiry of about 200 and by over 100 questionnaires filled out by widely separated individuals. One said he was sorry he had taken the drugs but then stated they had done him no harm, but that he now prefers alcohol. Another, who suffered a severe breakdown, was very appreciative of the role of the drugs in helping him face his problems. His was the only case requiring extended hospitalization.
9. St. Augustine, *Confessions,* trans. J. G. Pilkington (New York: Boni & Liveright, 1927), p. 229.
10. Studies by Father T. V. Moore, a generation ago, demonstrated that the risk of mental illness was greater among cloistered religious in "Insanity in Priests and Religious," *American Ecclesiastical Review* (1936), pp. 485-498.
11. See S. Cohen, "LSD: Side Effects and Complications," *Journal of Nervous and Mental Disease,* 130 (1960), pp. 30-40, for incidence of psychoses and suicides in experimental programs. An office manager at the psychological section of the Haight-Ashbury Medical Clinic told me that during her one to two years in charge she had known of *only two cases* of users of LSD who required hospitalization. She estimated incidence at somewhere between one in 500 to one in 1,000 of those seeking help. Doubtless much of this favorable record was due to the skill of clinic personnel. But it clearly points away from the exaggerated scare stories about LSD featured by most commonly accepted antidrug programs, even when it is used as casually as it is at Haight-Ashbury. However, careful studies are badly needed in this area.
12. For his theories, see T. Leary, *High Priest,* or better, *The Politics of Ecstasy* (New York: Putnam's, 1968), p. 136.

13. S. Cohen, *op. cit.* In personal conversation in 1968 Dr. Cohen stated to me that he had no reason for believing that a similar investigation would show different results today.

14. Dr. Werner Koella of the Worcester Foundation for Experimental Biology.

14A. J. H. Tjio, W. N. Pahnke, and A. A. Kurland, *Advances in Biochemical Psychopharmacology*, E. Costa and P. Greengard, eds. (New York: Raven Press, 1969), pp. 191-204.

15. It is of interest to note here that Dr. Herman Lisco of Harvard Medical School assayed chromosome breakages in the blood of Dr. Timothy Leary. He reported to Dr. Leary that his chromosomes were normal. Interested persons will find pertinent research reviewed in the February, 1968 *Bulletin* (#22) of the Psychedelic Information Center directed by Lisa Bieberman, 26 Boylston St., Suite 3, Cambridge, Mass. 02138. The *Bulletin*, published every two months, is free to those who send stamped, self-addressed envelopes. A review of research on chemical sources of possible genetic damage will be found in two articles on "Chemical Mutagens" by H. J. Sanders, in the May 19 and June 2, 1969, issues of *Chemical and Engineering News*. LSD is included along with other non-psychedelic drugs, some, like caffeine, in very common use. The Student Society for the Study of Hallucinogens at Beloit College, Beloit, Wisconsin, has a library of research articles and bibliographies available to members. Write for information.

9. The Psychedelics, the Law and the Inquisitor*

(It is) the eager sense of duty, zeal for sacrifice, and love of virtue, with the deadly taint of a conscience perverted by authority, which makes them so odious to touch and so curious to study.
        —Lord Acton[1]

We shall require them to turn upwards the vision of their souls and fix their gaze on that which sheds light on all, and when they have thus beheld the good itself they shall use it as a pattern for the right ordering of the state.
        —Plato[2]

The fact that the psychedelic chemicals have religious properties enormously complicates the problem of devising proper laws relative to their use and abuse. The problem derives largely from two sources: the United States Constitution, along with those of other democratic states, guarantees to its citizens freedom of religion, and the consciences of those who have deeply held religious beliefs seldom acknowledge the priority of man-made authority over their own religious convictions.

Some of the aims of this chapter will be: to help the reader understand more clearly the response of the religious person to laws that threaten his religious integrity; to consider the ability of magistrates and juries to empathize with religiously motivated offenders against the drug laws; to consider the character and

* Parts of this chapter reprinted with permission from the author's article, "Religious Aspects of Psychedelic Drugs," © California Law Review, 56, No. 1 (Jan., 1968), pp. 86-99.

role of the inquisitor as it may throw light on contemporary problems; against a background of the foregoing, to point out the need to diminish the fears of authorities, legislators and the public if conditions leading to witch-hunts and the police state are to be avoided; and to consider the role that religious experience such as that released by the drugs may play in affairs of the state.

Historical Instances of Resistance by Religious People. One of the persistent problems facing secular authority has always been the tendency of religious people to defy and disobey the law under certain circumstances. Those unsympathetic with such religious convictions have usually ascribed to such people fanaticism, lunacy, cowardice or some other form of social perversity, which may sometimes be the case. But it is difficult for contemporaries, without the benefit of history, to determine the wholesomeness of belief and behavior. Many of the world's greatest religious figures were once considered criminal, mad or both. Moses was a fugitive; the early Christians were accused of "hatred of the human race"; while Jeremiah suffered a variety of punishments for being on the wrong side of political opinion. The Book of Daniel and the Book of Revelation were designed to encourage those persecuted for their religious beliefs to stand fast.

The religious integrity of George Fox sent him to prison many times. The Albigenses, the Lollards and the Waldenses were hunted people, since their heretical beliefs threatened authority. Indeed, one of the main threats of the Waldenses derived from the fact that they were so "good"![3] Martin Luther took his historic stand in the shadow of martyrdom, while Sir Thomas More lost his head when he set the authority of God over the authority of his king. Today we have conscientious objectors who have chosen prison rather than the draft, and we have watched the pathetic instance of the Amish who have preferred to sell their ancestral lands rather than to send their children to schools subversive of the tenets of their faith.

In such cases the position of the law, supported by public opinion, finds an echo in a second century document concerning Christians written by Pliny, Roman Governor of Bithynia, to his master, the emperor Trajan. Pliny gave those culprits who confessed Christianity a chance to recant. "Those who persisted I ordered to be executed, for I did not doubt that whatever it was they professed they deserved to be punished for their inflexible obstinacy."[4]

In the history of religious persecution, mystics have always been conspicuous for the steadfastness of their beliefs, largely because the mystical conciousness is so much more deeply rooted than any other human impulse and is characterized by an experience that goes beyond death. These children of the second birth are particularly galling to the authorities, since they will meet death, if they must, with an equanimity that disturbs their judges and executioners with a sense of the limitations of their own power. It is always more comfortable to have such people out of the way.

One of the famous confrontations between an ecstatic and his accusers was that of Socrates and the Athenian electorate. Following an experience of illumination while on a military campaign, Socrates had become the leader of a group of young Athenians who idled away their time in talk, to the distress of the "more solid" citizens. Eventually, Socrates was brought to trial by his critics on charges that included that of corrupting the youth. Though confident of his ability to confound his accusers, Socrates was found guilty and condemned to death. One of the youth whom Socrates had "corrupted" was the writer of *The Republic.*

For Plato the greatest tragedy of his life was the execution of the wisest man he had ever known, and *The Republic* was his conception of a state in which such things could not happen. A central point was the sifting of the citizens to insure that the rulers would be philosophers illuminated by the kind of wisdom possessed by Socrates. In the famous Allegory of the Cave in the Seventh Book of *The Republic,* Plato makes it clear that this wisdom was of a mystical nature. Thus he gave an indirect indication that the decision against Socrates was a result of the failure of Socrates to communicate with the Athenian citizenry, who could not appreciate his point of view, because they had never participated in his kind of illumination. The older generation could not communicate with the younger generation, the hippies and the dropouts of the day.

In another day and under very different circumstances the same tragedy was played out in the medieval pursuit of those mystics whose words offended the conceptions of theological dogma and decorum. One of the most notable of these was the Dominican, Meister Eckhart, whose bold introspection into his own profound mystical states was labeled heresy, though only after his death, when punishment could no longer touch him. His heresy was that of Pantheism, though systematic examination of the utterances of other mystics are a tribute to the accuracy with which he described a state of mind, which he shared with many other notable religious spirits, both Christian and non-Christian.[5] If his theological judges had been able to understand him, they would have identified his consciousness with that of the great church fathers.

The boldness with which the mystic often asserts his convictions is also illustrated by an otherwise more docile spirit, Blessed Angela of Foligno, an influential thirteenth century Italian ecstatic. When she was informed by her directors that her charity and consequent love of poverty were too radical, she exclaimed, "Lord, even if I am damned, I will nevertheless do penance and will strip myself of everything and serve Thee!"[6] St. John of the Cross was also misunderstood by his ecclesiastical superiors, whom he resisted on more than one occasion.

In our own day, harassment of the Native American Church has proceeded in large measure from the failure of the government agents and missionaries to understand the state of mind of Indians who partake of peyote in their night-long ceremonies. It has been assumed that it was much like drunkenness, and that orgies with mental and moral degeneration necessarily followed. It has been chiefly the court testimony of disinterested anthropologists and other scientists that has preserved for these Indians their constitutional freedom to worship in their own way. Nevertheless, in small ways the peyote religion is still being persecuted through arrests and the passage of laws impeding the supply of sacramental substances.

On the whole, the mystics have played an important and honorable role in the development of the principle of religious freedom. They have made it clear that they will suffer harassment, imprisonment and even death to maintain their right to worship according to their consciences. Some of the bloodiest wars and massacres of history have involved campaigns against groups of mystics, and it has gradually dawned on mankind that humane and civilized practice involves respect for religious ways different from one's own.

The Religious Motive in Today's Resistance to the Drug Laws. Persecution is far from being a dead letter. The harassment of Dr. Timothy Leary, described in an earlier chapter, is a case in point. The pursuit and jailing of many hippies, their arrest on trivial charges and entrapment by spies is another example. Laws set penalties far beyond the reasonable, considering the nature of the "crime" committed, often that of unknowingly being in a place where illegal drugs are kept. While many of these offenders may not be motivated by anything more praiseworthy than a desire for thrills, there are others who consider the drugs a road to religious experience and a more effective life. This multiplies the resolve to defy the law. For example, the Reverend Arthur Kleps, Chief of the Neo-American Church, the white church incorporated for the purpose of pursuing the religious quest through drugs, testified before a Special Senate Judiciary Subcommittee on Narcotics on May 25, 1966. In part he said, "We are not drug addicts. We are not criminals. We are free men, and we will react to persecution the way free men have always reacted to persecution." There is no doubt that many see the pursuit of the religious quest through the use of the drugs as their legal right, and they will continue to use them regardless of conflict with the law.

Considerations such as these place the advocate of government by law in a dilemma. No one denies the right to freedom of religion in principle, but the campaign against the drugs assumes abuse of the drugs. While most law enforcement officers either do not know that the psychedelics have religious properties or disbelieve it, this fact is gradually being brought to their attention. However, they will still make the points that the drugs are much too dangerous for religious people to use, and that those wholly devoid of religious motive will simply use religion as a cloak for irresponsible indulgence.

Arguments like these, logically extended, would enable the authorities to ban or prevent from the beginning almost any religious group of which they disapproved. One could hardly deny the possibility that irresponsible people might abuse their right of freedom of religion and use the drugs in such a way as to do harm. Any freedom may be abused. And certainly even freedom of religion is not absolute, for an acknowledged premise is that the exercise of a particular religious rite must not do harm to others or offend grossly against society's sense of decency. For example, the plea of religious freedom would hardly excuse a rite of human sacrifice, while actual precedents pretty generally accepted are the laws against polygamy. The law has the right and duty to police such matters.

But a man is assumed innocent until he is proved guilty. An extension of this principle would seem to protect unusual types of religious worship until they not only have been proved harmful but also more harmful than they are good. A *completely* harmless religion, it may be noted, is an ineffective one. If it was regularly found that the administration of the psychedelic sacrament was accompanied by several suicides and people jumping off the church roof—a sequel, incidentally, which would not surprise the average newspaper reader—then a ban on psychedelic churches would be in order. If this was not true, a blanket law would not be warranted, although the closing of particular churches might be justified when irresponsibility could be demonstrated.

Furthermore, it is extremely unlikely that abuses would be greater than the benefits. Institutions tend to be conservative, and psychedelic churches would be especially careful to screen recipients of the sacrament and to take other safeguards in the interest of their worshippers and the continuance of their own rights when they realized that their privileges rested on responsible use of the chemicals. In the only psychedelic church now publicly tolerated, the Native American Church, accidents are few or nonexistent, while benefits are many. In a responsible church like the Church of the Awakening, it would be surprising to find any abuse. Indeed, I would be surprised if there were any serious trouble. In any case, lawmakers have no right to assume abuse *a priori*.

A more debatable issue is whether individuals should be allowed to use the drugs apart from a supervising body, if such use was sincerely religious. Here I am doubtful, since there is no question but that an experienced guide is essential for maximizing benefits and minimizing dangers. This desirable condition can easily be fulfilled under open but controlled use, whether for therapeutic or religious purposes. This would point to the need for some form of group use, as with a church body. On the other hand, I do know of some cases where the drugs have been used with sincere religious intent and with seemingly great benefit by individuals. One such person undergoes the LSD ordeal as a matter of principle and discipline three times a year. In *The Politics of Ecstasy*,[7] Dr. Leary lays down the maxim that nobody should force others to alter their consciousness, and no one should prevent another from doing the same, providing others are not harmed thereby. He advocates personal licensing as a means of control. But here the courts and legislative bodies would have to decide. I am simply registering my preference for skilled and experienced administration of psychedelic drugs under all circumstances.

Law Enforcement and the Concept of the Inquisitor. Human nature does not change, generally speaking. Consequently, though history never repeats itself in each little detail, one of the benefits that a study of history confers is that of perspective. There are certain historical regularities that are profitable to note.

One of the repeating phenomena of history is the presence and role of the inquisitor. Here I wish to detach the reader from what is probably his settled picture of the inquisitor as an ogre with blood lust, a caricature emphasizing the most unlovely and revolting characteristics of the type. Indeed, the inquisitor is always with us, inside each of us, and up to a point, desirably so. Probably I am doing an injustice to the memory of many a conscientious inquisitorial churchman who does not deserve the opprobrium that, since medieval times, has been attached to his function. But I wish to point out the danger we are always in of allowing our zeal for "doing good" and protecting the public to run away with our feelings, often perverting both justice and humane considerations through a hysteria implemented by officials seduced by a sense of power.

The roots of inquisitorial cruelty are to be found in the necessity of ordering any institutional structure, but especially a state or quasi state, like the church of the Middle Ages, where the power exercised in certain areas is absolute. Here any feeling of weakness or insecurity is apt to be turned into unreasonable demands, usually well rationalized and based on impeccable logic.[8] The greater the fear aroused in the authorities, and the more conscientious they are, the more unreasonable and drastic the punishments, generally speaking. Such a condition was present during the early Christian era, and it should be noted that on the whole it was the more conscientious Roman emperors, essentially inquisitors in the sense I have given the term, who insisted on compliance with the state religion under the pain of death.[9]

But the medieval inquisitor, who is the focus of my comparison, was a sincere, conscientious, responsible, well-educated man, concerned for the welfare of the people, sometimes even compassionate, though also a creature of logic in pursuit of the letter of the law. He was not popularly regarded as a man devoid of human sympathy. On the contrary, he was regarded with veneration. He was likely to be enthusiastic and hard working, believing himself a servant of God. If he was cruel, this stemmed from the terrible logic of his position and showed itself in colors of stark terror chiefly to his victims, while the populace in general looked on him as their protector. He was a man of affairs, not a fanatic. The words of Lord Acton, though used with a different application, are appropriate to the inquisitors of all ages. It is a combination of "eager sense of duty, zeal for sacrifice, and love of virtue, with the deadly taint of a conscience perverted by authority, which makes them so odious to touch and so curious to study."[10]

Even the notorious Torquemada did not differ markedly from this description, though he was doubtless more bigoted and cruel than the general run. But a fairer representative was the able Franciscan, Cardinal Ximenes, appointed Inquisitor General of Spain by King Ferdinand in 1507. An anchorite who darned his own habit and slept on the floor, he was a man of absolute probity and integrity. He was prevailed on to assume the ornate symbols of his rank only by the command of the pope. He was zealous to protect the purity of the Catholic faith that men might go to heaven rather than to hell; therefore, the hunting down and burning alive of thousands of Jews, Moors, and heretics to the glory of God.[11]

It is particularly instructive to examine the inquisitors' treatment of witchcraft. Under the impact of the study of science, witchcraft has now almost completely died out, at least among the educated; but our American forefathers also indulged in campaigns against presumed witches. Though witchcraft and sorcery were generally believed, and even semirespectable in the 13th century, in the 16th and 17th they were discredited and identified with heathenism and the work of the devil, though still feared. It was principally this fear that loosed the panic legislation and hunting of witches by Catholics and Protestants alike. Witchcraft, which had been practiced openly by certain people, was driven underground, compounding the hysteria. This necessitated a complicated system of spying, with the rise of a special class of professional informers and *agents provocateurs*. Every man suspected his neighbor, and in some towns the reputation of no woman was safe.

We are told, for example, that in the city of Arras in 1459-1460 A.D., the accusation of one alleged witch touched off a series of accusations and hysteria that nearly ruined the city. The inquisitor, doubtless sincere and disinterested, was "genuinely aghast . . . at the evil . . . blind to the fact that its magnitude was mainly of his own creation."[12] Furthermore, the Inquisition's concern to root out witchcraft bears much of the blame for spreading it. It probably would have died a quiet death with the passage of time had it been let alone. As in the case of much heresy, suspicion was cast on any one whose behavior departed from the social norm. This included many sincere ecstatics and mystics whose integrity was sensed by empathic and sensitive authorities. But few secular magistrates were willing to undergo the spiritual and material risk of excommunication "for the sake of a few fanatical schismatics."[13]

Advantaged as we are through the perspective that history gives us, and pretty well freed from the partisanship and hysteria of those times, it is easy for us to see that something was wrong. We have decided that society is not well protected by the burning alive of witches and heretics nor is God glorified thereby, no matter how well meaning and responsible the agents of such a policy.

It is not so easy to detect symptoms of similar fallacies in our times, because our own variety of fears involves practices about whose danger we are as certain as medieval citizens were sure of the dangers of heresy. We can abhor the shadowy figure of the inquisitor, as we can the Nazi storm trooper; but we can hardly empathize with him, since to do so would be too threatening to our own self-esteem. This is a pity, not just because mistaken men, like us, deserve compassion, but because it prevents our detecting the inquisitor residing deeply within ourselves. If we recognized him, the resulting humility might prevent our making the same mistakes our predecessors made in half-forgotten times. It might give our legislators, enforcement officers, civic leaders, and self-appointed "experts" on drug effects protection from overuse of the punitive function of the law as a means of social control.

Doubtless it will help each individual to recognize his own personal internal inquisitor if I rehabilitate somewhat the inquisitorial personality, then differentiate it from the personality of what, for want of a better term, we might call the personality of "the saint." I am using the concept of saintliness loosely in the sense of William James in *The Varieties of Religious Experience,* as I did in discussing the personality of Timothy Leary in an earlier chapter and I am remembering that saints may be guilty of their own type of excesses. Each of us harbors his own internal saint as well as his inquisitor.

Hence, we may think of the inquisitor as a person with a concern for the collective welfare, while the saint is more disposed toward respect for the individual. Cain asked, "Am I my brother's keeper?" The inquisitor answers, "Yes." The saint, though not in Cain's spirit, sees his duty as that of freeing his brother from the shackles of social custom. The inquisitor is keenly aware of his responsibility for public order and the curbing of the vicious, the greedy and the irresponsible. The saint feels he has the higher responsibility for maintaining conditions of creative freedom. The inquisitor says, "No, No!" The saint says, "Yes, Yes!" At his best, the inquisitor is noted for his even-handed administration of justice, the saint for compassion.

Assuming the correctness of my hasty picture, it is easy to see that the virtures of the inquisitorial type are needed by society, and in some form are part of everyone's personality. What I have described is a necessary part of the psychological equipment of every public authority and every administrator. The problem is to see that these virtues do not get out of hand.

That the virtues of the inquisitor have gotten out of hand in the campaign against drug abuse, and that the authorities are most clamorous in the area of the psychedelics—not the most dangerous category—seems clear. More tragedies have occurred through breaking the laws against the psychedelics, arrest, consequent imprisonment and criminal records than in any abuse.

I have been told that 6,000 convicts in the prisons of California alone are there for violations of the narcotics laws. Even if we assume this is an overestimate and that only a few of these are there for abuse of marihuana and LSD, we are still faced with the tragedy of the ruination of many careers, not to speak of the degradation of hundreds of gentle and idealistic young lives.[14] Can those who advocate harsh, punitive restrictions on the psychedelics, including their religious use, point to hard evidence of equally numerous tragedies resulting from abuse? Still there are cries for yet more punishment and stricter, rather than more selective and humane enforcement, in a situation where the cure is already far more frightful than the disease. And still there are those who for religion's sake will persist in using these drugs because their consciences tell them that they must. These must be dealt with in some civilized and constructive way.

Perhaps the reader has already seen parallels between the inquisition and the campaign against drugs. We have exaggerated penalties for supposed crimes against the community through the use of drugs that have not yet been proved to be addictive or even harmful, as with marihuana. We have the planting of spies, raids by police in the dead of night, the entrapment of violators through the use of *agents provocateurs*. All of these practices are reminiscent of the inquisition as well as the modern police state. I know of the case of a refined young woman, ignorant of the law, tricked into sending LSD through the mails to a narcotics agent posing as a religious seeker. Because she is a convicted criminal, she is now unable to procure an automobile license in her home state, not to speak of potentially more serious disabilities further on in her career.

In Massachusetts there have been arrests and prison sentences for the felony of (unknowingly) being found in places where marihuana was kept. In California life imprisonment may be given for violation of many of the statutes against the use of marihuana, even, in certain circumstances, for possession for one's own use. In the state of Georgia the penalty for selling marijuana to a minor, second offense, is mandatory death! Dr. Leary was given a sentence of thirty years and a $30,000 fine, reversed by the U.S. Supreme Court in May, 1969, on a violation chiefly technical. Even the inquisition could hardly be considered much harsher than this. Furthermore, the net result of such punitive practices seems to have been the stimulation of irresponsible use of drugs rather than the reverse. The situation is rife with fear, suspicion and defiance.

There is, of course, a means whereby an insistent authority can get its way. There are administrators to whom any threat to law is a threat to themselves. With sufficient force behind them and a single-minded determination to maintain authority at any cost, the job can be done. With energy lent by religious motivation, human nature may be amazingly resistant and troublesome to even the most awesome authority. But rebellion has been crushed, and those who insist that only repressive laws inexorably enforced will solve the drug problem will find an instructive example in the suppression of the heresy of the Catharists or Albigensians in southern France of the Middle Ages. The heresy was not a very appealing one, but the ruthlessness with which it was put down ended its threat to the church for all time. For example, after the taking of the town of Beziers, practically the whole population was put to the sword, including some faithful Catholics, lest any heretic escape.[15] How far are those who uphold "law and order" willing to go in emulating such logic?

So far the punitive fury of those entrusted with the duty of enforcement has fallen far short of this intensity, and it must be said that there are many wise and compassionate judges and narcotics agents. But there is a point beyond which there is no return for a frightened populace. This will make any humane concession to either human weakness or steadfast principle seem a hazard for those enforcing the laws. Such signs of police state methods as I have noted suggest a failure of nerve, which does not bode well for the future, unless somehow the present trends are reversed.

Conclusion. It is much easier to point out weaknesses than to suggest satisfactory ways of handling complex problems. I am not trained in the law and have no special competence in the legal area. What I do have is a lifelong interest in the subject of religious experience and its effects on people, and eight years of direct research and extensive study of the religious properties of the psychedelic chemicals. It is from this background that I suggest the following changes in social policy and laws relating to this particular classification of drugs:

1. *Distinguish the psychedelics from the addictive drugs like the opiates, amphetamines, and alcohol.* When, for example, LSD is placed in the same category with heroin as a "hard drug," and then youths find that many can use LSD extensively with no apparent bad effects, it is easier for them to assume that the same is true of these other more dangerous drugs.

2. *Abandon the policy of trying to scare young people by telling them only the dangers of the drugs,* as does a popular film on LSD entitled "Insight or Insanity." Rushing into print with hasty reports of damage to the chromosomes of LSD users, or downright hoaxes like the story of the four students blinded by looking at the sun on an LSD trip are ineffectual and unjust. In the long run, youth will jump to the conclusion that their elders are either ignorant or lying to them. In either case, they will dismiss the good along with the bad. There are better reasons than these for being careful with LSD, and ultimately society has much more to gain by keeping lines of communication open, whether to guide the younger generation or to learn from them. Here, as elsewhere, if it is an effective policy we are after, we can repeat the old maxim, "Honesty is the best policy."

3. *Repeal all laws for possession of the psychedelic drugs (as*

distinct from their sale); rationalize and humanize other restrictive laws relative to their use. This would reduce much of the spying on drug users, their suspicion and often furious, though repressed, resentment against law enforcers. At the same time, fewer narcotics agents would be needed, and those retained would be forced to focus their enforcement duties where it belongs and where maximum benefits will be secured, namely, on the curbing of large-scale manufacturers and distributors of illicit drugs.

4. *Set up government sponsored or government licensed psychedelic clinics staffed with experts where people who wish to take the psychedelic drugs for any reason may apply.* First they would be given up-to-date information on the effects of the drugs and receive proper screening. We are often told of the great need of sound information about the drugs through reliable research. Here would be an opportunity to obtain such information. We are already greatly concerned about the number of individuals experimenting on themselves. Here would be a chance to make some constructive use of this experimentation in an environment which would minimize dangers and maximize benefits by the use of reliable drugs, dosage and proper support.

5. *Supplement the foregoing program with government licensing for specially trained psychiatrists and psychologists to use the psychedelic drugs in their practice and research.* This is the method used in Czechoslovakia, the country which has perhaps the most rational and successful method of controlling and using the drugs. The problem of psychedelic drug abuse in Czechoslovakia is said to be minimal, if not nonexistent. There are many experienced therapists in this country whose patients have profited from their effective use of LSD-type drugs. These therapists are skilled in their use. It is a social waste and an unwarranted interference with their professional competence to deny them access to these chemicals.

6. *Permission should be given to properly incorporated religious institutions to use the drugs in worship.* This permission would be revoked only after *proved* and *persistent* evidence of abuse of this permission. This safeguard of freedom of religion already exists with respect to the Native American Church. There is no evidence that there is any large scale abuse of the permission, if any. A man is assumed innocent until he can be proved guilty. By an extension of a similar principle, it should be assumed that the psychedelic churches will be exercising their right to freedom of religion until it can be proved that their worship in some way is a serious threat to society, cancelling the good.

Alterations of our treatment of drugs offenders, as suggested above, would not automatically and overnight solve all society's problems with reference to this troubled scene. But it would mitigate some of its worst abuses. At the same time, it would start a movement away from what many of our most sensitive observers see as a dangerous drift in the direction of the police state. The subtle progress of the everpresent temptation to save society by following in the footsteps of the inquisition will not be halted until he recognizes the inquisitor in himself. He who does not recognize that he has offended by impulse or by act at some point in his career is in danger of repeating history's mistakes. The most loathed, hated and feared of the worst human qualities that history can show us sleep within ourselves, just as the best do, too. It is time for us to take stock of the road on which we are traveling if we are not some day to find ourselves in the nightmare society of George Orwell's Big Brother.

Furthermore, if the insights of Plato have anything of value for modern political science it is that the illumination of those who have escaped the restricted vision of the dark Cave of Illusion is necessary for any proper ordering of the state. This illumination is universal and noncreedal, but in its essence it is deeply religious. Those who have had wide experience with people who have ingested the psychedelics know that many have had their lives enriched by such religious perceptions. The drugs are not the only road to religion, but there are millions of Americans who either will know religion through the agency of the drugs, or they will never know it at all. Have our lawmakers and magistrates the wisdom and inner authority, which gives them the right to deny to citizens this road to the inner vision? The only hope, not only of America alone but the world state as well— if we can trust Plato—lies in rulers selected for many qualities, but chiefly because they experienced in some way this transcendental vision of the Good.

Summary. In this chapter I have tried to put certain of the legal aspects, particularly those of a religious nature, posed by society's attack on the drug problem, in historical perspective. I have done this by pointing out that the deeply religious motive has never subordinated itself to law, partly because it has sensed that its accusers have not properly understood it. This has often led to the punishment and execution of humanity's most perceptive spirits, particularly the mystics, in history's most tragic encounters. Such tragedies have led to the development of the principle of freedom of religion.

I have then tried to show that at least some of present day offenders against the drugs laws have shown every evidence of being motivated by the same type of stubborn religious conviction, and they have been met with the same variety of repression. I have briefly tried to show certain similarities to one of history's worst persecutions, the inquisition of the Middle Ages. By trying to show the reader that the chief agents of the inquisition were not monsters but conscientious human beings attempting to protect society, I have suggested that conscientious citizens of the present day who are campaigning against drug abuse may be following the same road and unwittingly perpetrating an offense that is much worse than the abuses they are trying to correct.

Lawmakers must, of course, be guided not only by scientific findings but also by all facets of the psychedelics. Their most subtle and puzzling aspect is their religious agency. As a psychologist of religion, I have been impressed by the fact that these drugs, handled correctly, appear to offer incomparable opportunities for studying religious experience. Religious experience is the most profound and powerful aspect of the human personality and is the aspect most capable of bringing out the compassionate and creative qualities of the human spirit. Furthermore, it is the most effective agent of wholesome, profound personality change. The law can maximize or minimize the value of drugs for religion. It can also make the mistake of persecuting men who are merely attempting to experience that part of their nature that they feel most entitles them to regard themselves as human, namely, their encounter with Ultimate Reality, or what they call God.

In pursuit of such encounter religious people have felt compelled to defy the law when lawmakers have misunderstood their basic urge. Education, common intelligence, integrity and judgment alone are not enough to deal with such energies and perceptions as are loosed in the saints. This is one of the lessons that the inquisition has for the present day. But it will require rare introspective ability to sense that each one of us has a potential inquisitor hidden within us. More than this, we will require wisdom to cast off the chains that fetter us in the dark Cave of Illusion if we are to encounter the sunlight, which, for Plato, must enlighten those few fit to judge and govern the state.

NOTES

1. Lord Acton, quoted in G. S. Coulton, *Inquisition and Liberty* (London: Heineman, 1938), p. 167.
2. Plato, *The Republic*, Seventh Book.
3. A. S. Turberville, *Medieval Heresy and the Inquisition* (London: Archon, 1964), p. 22.
4. Quoted in R. Bainton, *The Horizon History of Christianity* (New York: American Heritage Publishing Co., 1964), pp. 66-67.
5. See W. T. Stace, *Mysticism and Philosophy* (Philadelphia: Lippincott, 1960).
6. Quoted in W. H. Clark, *The Psychology of Religion* (New York: Macmillan, 1958), p. 288.
7. Timothy Leary, *The Politics of Ecstasy* (New York: G. P. Putnam's Sons, 1968), pp. 69, 95.
8. See G. S. Coulton, *Inquisition and Liberty* (London: Heineman, 1938), p. 167, and Turberville, *Medieval Heresy and the Inquisition*, pp. 178-179.
9. See article on Pliny The Younger, *Encyclopedia Britannica* (1929), for correspondence with Emperor Trajan and the relatively restrained and principled views of the latter as compared with the popular Christian image of the bloodthirsty Roman in the times of the persecutions.
10. Quoted in Coulton, *Inquisition and Liberty*, p. 167.
11. For a brief biographical study of Ximenses, see J. Plaidy, *The Growth of the Spanish Inquisition* (London: Robert Hale, Ltd., 1960), chaps. 2-5.
12. Turberville, *Medieval Heresy and the Inquisition*, p. 122. Information in this part of the chapter largely derived from Turberville, p. 111 ff, and Coulton, *Inquisition and Liberty*, p. 262 ff.
13. Turberville, *Medieval Heresy and the Inquisition*, p. 157.
14. According to J. T. Carey, Prof. of Criminology, University of California, Berkeley, arrests for state narcotics violations in California during the first half of 1967 involving marihuana alone were: adults, 11,587; juveniles 4,526, in "Marihuana among the New Bohemians," *Journal of Psychedelic Drugs*, 2, no. 1 (Fall, 1968), p. 80.
15. See Turberville, *op. cit.*, pp. 14 ff., 123 ff; Coulton, *op. cit.*, chap. 9.

10. Conclusions and Prescriptions

One must still have chaos within oneself in order to give birth to a dancing star. —Friedrich Nietzsche[1]

Verily, verily, I say unto thee, unless a man be born again he cannot enter the Kingdom of God. —Jesus of Nazareth[2]

I am not a pharmacologist but a psychologist of religion. Neither am I a mystic, but a scholar of religion and a believer in the importance of mysticism. I have tried to present my subject systematically, judiciously and as sympathetically as I could. But at best I have penetrated but a little way into the vast expanses of the inner world. From my own experience I know only a little of the mysteries, terrors, joys and rewards that lie hidden in its distances. On the basis of such glimpses as I have had, the vast reaches of these undiscovered wilds are awesome.

Those who, without the help of LSD, have already "been there," need no drug. There are other roads if one has time, persistence and membership in the brotherhood of those who "hunger and thirst after righteousness" to whom the Scriptures have promised, "they shall be filled." Most of what I have learned about religion at first hand I have learned from my encounter with the psychedelics. I speak advisedly, deliberately and thoughtfully. As a scholar, I have learned at least as much, though not more, from my six "trips" as I have from all the plodding study in my field of the psychology of religion. The two are differing roads which complement one another.

155

In the psychedelic field such benefits can no more be guaranteed than they can in any other creative adventure. One must find the proper opportunity and guide, study all sides of the subject, then decide whether to take the calculated risk all religion worth the name requires. Some of the warnings against the journey are terrifying, and one is well advised not to encounter the adventure unsupplied with a cool and resolute nerve. The journey is not for the unstable and the timid unless under the direction of an exceptionally well-trained and empathic specialist.[3] Whether the encounter is with heaven or with hell, it can hardly fail to provide insight, self-knowledge and growth. With proper motivation it may turn out to be life-changing in nature—an "ego death" with consequent rebirth.

"Except a man be born again he cannot see the kingdom of God," said Jesus to the bewildered Nicodemus. This is exactly what some favored spirits have reported through the drugs. They have found their lives by losing them. It is for these reasons that neither scholarship nor religious study, neither the university nor the church, nor the scientist, nor the artist, the educator, the prophet, nor the mystic can neglect informing himself of the opportunities for personal growth available through chemical ecstasy. At the very least, the inquiry requires a careful weighing of the facts, an unwillingness to be satisfied by social or scientific clichés about the matter. In a time of such hysteria over a controversial subject, the true intellectual and religious inquirer cannot rely on information from others, not even the most scientific hearsay. He dare not refuse to look for himself through Galileo's telescope.

Failing this measure of scientific intrepidity, he can at least be discriminating in choosing his informants, his experts. These will not be physicians who have merely witnessed frightening panics among those who have taken the drugs or who have cared for those with extended disturbances. Even though such things occur only rarely, they do occur and must be taken into consideration in any overall estimate of the advisability of psychedelic usage.[4] But one should be cautious in accepting the views of *anyone* in this field unless he is a true expert who has observed many drug administrations (at least 100) from beginning to end, has engaged in systematic follow-up of these and other cases; and has experimented on himself, preferably with several ingestions. In other words, he must have "been there" himself. This type of expert is most likely to have a balanced picture of benefits and of dangers and to understand the experience of others.

I have said that this is a book on religion. My focus is religion, not the drugs. I have given the evidence in previous chapters that persuades me of the religious agency of the drugs: ingesters have reported the characteristics of profound mystical experience; they speak of "death and rebirth," "redemption," "salvation," the "white light," the "dazzling darkness," perhaps that "dark silence in which all lovers lose themselves," in which the words of Scripture and religious ecstasy come alive. Love is transformed from a cliché to a living and vital reality. Lifelong, obdurate convicts have become compassionate, and near-delinquents have been gentled. It is reported that Kenneth Kesey took Hell's Angels into the country and gave them LSD. When I visited Haight-Ashbury, one hippie told me, "We used to be afraid of them, but now they protect us!"[5]

This is not to say that changes in personality brought about through the drugs may not develop their own problems, but it is worth noting that the development of empathy, compassion and love, and the substitution of understanding and communication for hatred and violence is the religious message that comes closest to uniting all religious faiths. In all ages and all faiths it has been found that such are the results of the ecstatic, mystical experience, wherever it is found and however it may be triggered. It is significant that it was a mystic who wrote, "Send not to enquire for whom the bell tolls; it tolls for thee."

For this reason the religious "establishment" dare not avoid facing the issues raised by the drugs without laying themselves open to the charge that they are neglecting the very roots of faith. But it often seems that there is nothing that the churches fear so much as religion! Yet if violence is the root of both external and internal threat, and if religion considers itself a means of combatting violence, then it has an obligation to examine the claims of those who promote chemical ecstasy as a means of saving the nation and saving the world. In these days of peril, no religious leader can afford to overlook *any source* of religious motivation, no matter how strange, and particularly one that in so many cases has proved effective.

I have several times made the point that there are many roads to religious ecstasy. Sensory deprivation and fasting, as anchorites have long known, meditation, a whirling dance, chanting, childbirth, closeness to nature, breathing exercises, concentrated attention, falling in love and physical exhaustion are some of the triggers that may cause those stirrings of the unconscious that may eventuate in ecstasy.[6] Many will contend that these are "safe" roads to religion, compared with the drugs, but this is an illusion. If religion is to be made safe, then it also must be made ineffective. The more powerful the religious impulse, the more potentially dangerous it will be.

It is clear that there are forms of the psychedelics that are very poisonous in themselves, like the *Amanita muscaria* mushroom and the jimson weed; but in agents like LSD, in usual dosages and so far as it has been proved to date, the danger seems to reside in the powerful experience itself, which is religious in its essence. Whoever attempts the awesome task of deliberately coming into the presence of God takes the risk, calculated or uncalculated, of experiencing madness. The *mysterium tremendum* of which Rudolf Otto speaks will warn him, if nothing else does. The same is true of other fields of creative ecstasy, or other means of releasing powerful feelings. A recent article warns of the need for caution among those interested in group therapy and sensitivity training.[7] The question is not whether ecstasy is risky, but whether the expected gains outweigh the risks. This is a matter which each individual must decide for himself, but society must make decisions when the individual may be endangering the welfare of others.

One of the important contributions of the drug movement to religion is that it has called the attention of religious people to the necessity of ecstasy for vital religion. More ministers and church members than the general public is aware of have tried the drugs and are only waiting for a favorable opportunity to say so. Furthermore, religious ecstasy was not discovered by the drug cults. It has been known for centuries, as I have tried to demonstrate.

There is no doubt that the drugs have introduced many of the youthful generation to a firsthand religious experience that they would have encountered in no other way. I have personally known of five atheists, and I have read of many more, whose respect for religion was conceived through the drugs. Two of these have been featured in this book. Not all who take the drugs continue in their use. There seems to be a tendency to give up LSD for other methods of pursuing the religious quest. Even those who have given them up have acknowledged the crucial agency of the drugs in a new religious birth. They are glad they took them.

We can go further than the religious sphere and see the need for ecstasy in all of life. This is the solid core of truth in the message of the hippies, who prefer a chaos with its promise and its dangers to a dull though safe routine sold out to vested interests, power and the greed for money. Nietzsche said that it requires a chaos to produce the "dancing star."[8]

Mankind may be divided into the participants and the observers. Most of us participate in some activity and observe the rest of life. Those who have been introduced to the realities of religious existence through drugs, and who have taken up the hippie way of life as a result tend to be participants in the spiritual life rather than observers of it. Many of them may fall short of their aims and become confused, but they are engaged in religious living more actively than the average churchgoer for whom religion has become formalized and a sideline, at best. This citizen in the same way becomes a taster of art and a patron of music. No matter how well educated he may be in his hobby, he is fundamentally an observer compared with the creators of great masterpieces, who have risked their careers, their lives and their very sanity in those gambles without which their masterpieces would never have come into being.

Our religions, our Great Society, our culture, and our civilization would be without even the pretense to greatness without ecstasy in some form. The common man may rub his eyes in utter disbelief when the true prophet appears. He may confuse him with the multitude of shallow ecstatics, deluded visionaries, lunatics, calculating seekers after money or power and plain ordinary fools. It is for this reason that so many great religious leaders cannot properly be estimated until after they are dead.

The effect of ecstasy of any variety is to create motivation, the longing to continue the ecstasy and fulfill it. Critics of the drug cults complain that they retreat from life's realities, become passive and inert. Actually, it is not so much this aspect of the psychedelic scene but its precise opposite to which they object. It is the activism and participation, the radical departure from cultural norms that frighten older people, the "straight" people and the "squares." It is not the *reading* of the works of Henry

David Thoreau, patron saint of the hippies; it is the *taking him seriously* to which society objects. How else can one explain the hue and cry, the harassment and the multiple arrests of Timothy Leary? It is not the disapproval of his "dropping out" that disturbs society; it is the fear that through his own radical break with current middle class values, religious and otherwise, he is "dropping in" to too many young lives, not just by his precept but by his example. Respectable society approves of art and religion in principle; but, like the apocryphal Englishmen amid the fall glory of Vermont foliage, it does not like to see them overdone.

Since I am speaking more as an observer than a participant, it is my duty to point to a few cautions to be kept in mind in dealing with this exceedingly complex scene. Two human polarities are those of the structured versus the expansive individual. The structured man is impressed by the need for system, organization, order and restraint. He is the classical person rather than the romantic, more realistic than fanciful. In religion he is the priest rather than the prophet, the theologian rather than the mystic. For any human activity to become effective, both of these two poles must be represented; but each has its legitimate function and each its besetting weaknesses. I have sung the praises of religious ecstasy long enough and so I must sound some warnings.

The ecstatic consciousness is an expansive consciousness, open to a profusion of new sensations, new perceptions, new knowledge and new values. It is this condition that tends to create confusion, or chaos lacking a governing order that will enable it to bear creative fruit. The raw and vital energies released through ecstasy must be directed in some way if they are not to become destructive and demonic. The structured and expansive functions require one another.

For this reason one may question the long-term wisdom of the tendency of so many of the drug takers to seek expression through religious traditions alien to their upbringing. The Hindu and Buddhist traditions are richer in the ways of mystical understanding and their followers adapt themselves to mystical expression better than the western faiths. If the religious vigor of a westerner is thereby enhanced, this is certainly preferable to a foolish allegiance to a dead faith.

Most westerners have been brought up with some roots in western faiths, whether Moslem, Jewish or Christian. All three of these faiths have their mystical traditions onto which the psychedelic ecstasy may be grafted. The historical tradition may then provide religious norms and values which constitute a great pool of religious wisdom built into the individual's mind and into his *feelings* as well. It is at the same time a touchstone of worth and a balance wheel against ecstatic explosions.

A second important caution is the warning against quietism. The life of the righteous requires a constant activism, and the danger that this may become a round of sterile busy-ness or empty piety is certainly great. Ecstatics may react against this by an emphasis on mysticism. However, ecstasy may become a habit of lazy self-indulgence. Paradoxically, the mystics have declared their experiences ineffable, but many then develop a tendency to excessive talk. It is easier for them to talk about love and the spiritual life than to demonstrate it.

Although there is no doubt that chemical ecstasy, like any other kind, tends to generate compassion, true compassion is an active principle, not a passive one. All things change, and history has never recorded a good movement that did not degenerate with time. Man was never meant to throw his brains away, and it is only a reflection of this kind, properly applied, that will save the psychedelic drug movement from itself. It needs self-criticism from within as much as it needs understanding from without.[9]

A cognate need is for continuing research in the drug field. It may be true that the impulses released by LSD, and sometimes even by marihuana, are holy. But I am not aware that God has declared Himself above being studied, so long as the study is carried out with reverence and concern for the feelings of those who are involved in the study. Pahnke's Good Friday experiment is a model. Furthermore, if there is hard evidence that the Native American Church, or any other cultic group, has been breeding a race of monsters and defectives as the result of using psychedelic substances over the centuries, any religious groups using the drugs will want to know it.

There is also need for more dedicated scientists willing to take the calculated risk of ingesting the psychedelics themselves for the sake of the understanding that such an experience will give them. Some scientists have boxed themselves into a logical corner by contending that the psychedelic experience deprives people of judgment, and so anyone who has had the experience is incompetent to study it. It is good that William James had no such scruples when he tried nitrous oxide, or we would be deprived of some of his most fertile insights into mysticism. Furthermore, there are many keen and fully critical intelligences who have profited from the drug experience. Their understanding was enhanced and illuminated by it. One is not disqualified as a critic of Freudianism through a personal psychoanalysis. It is true that many have become prophets and psychedelic evangelists through the drugs, but society needs its prophets as well as its scientists, even though both on occasion have been mistaken. However, the drug experimenters should keep in touch with the findings of science.

To come back to the issue of the stance of the established churches, it seems likely, as things stand at this writing, that any religious use of the drugs will have to be carried on in cults, outside traditional institutions. This is a pity, for it deprives the churches of the possibility of a powerful influx of ecstatic energy —the very element of which they are in shortest supply. Thus modern churchmen run the ancient risk of obstructionism. Eighteenth century churchmen criticised experiments with vaccination as blasphemous attempts to deprive God of his prerogative of punishing the wicked through smallpox, and it was dangerous for a God-fearing scientist to look through Galileo's telescope. Even in our own century teachers have been dismissed at the instance of the pious for declaring that creation took longer than six days!

Every ecstatic movement, starting long before Socrates and the ecstatic cults of Greece down to the Pentecostalism of the present day, had its critics who were contemporary defenders of the faith. The church has created schism rather than tolerate the vitalizing energies of the Waldensians, the Hussites, the Lutherans, the Anabaptists or the Wesleyans. Consequently, it is probably too much to expect in the present state of controversy over the drugs that any established religious institutions will officially authorize their religious use.

It is significant that at the same time that the Roman Catholic Church has closed its doors on ecstacy at one time in history, it has been tolerant and accepting at another. Francis, Loyola and Teresa were only three ecstatics whose movements started spontaneously and were opposed before they obtained the approval of the pope. One of the strengths of the Roman Church has been its ability from time to time, even though not always, to refresh its spiritual dynamic by accommodating itself to what some of the faithful thought were dangerous tendencies. Even today the movement of the worker priests abroad and the Catholic Worker movement in the United States are examples of tolerated groups whose vigor and radicalism most Catholics fear.

In some such way there may develop small enclaves of dedicated worshippers willing to face the risks of the drugs. They meet in homes or other modern equivalents of the catacombs to experiment with ecstasy through a judicious use of these powerful agencies. If such adventurers on the frontiers of spirituality, who still keep in touch with their primary religious institutions, can demonstrate the soundness of their methods, then perhaps they may some day be allowed to enrich timid churches through a new and vital strain.

In one way or another, it will be necessary for the churches to take some notice of the drug movement. Many members of churches and synagogues have already taken notice, have tried the drugs and have left their ancestral faiths, convinced that church leaders are too timid and too blind to recognize their own best interests. Eventually, the churches will be forced to take some sort of a stand. It is extremely important that such stands be taken out of knowledge and not out of ignorance. With a cautious boldness the churches must be willing to experiment themselves, for in some way they will have to come to terms with ecstasy. This issue has been raised by the religious usage of the psychedelic chemicals and has been posed in these pages.

NOTES

1. Friedrich Nietzsche, *An Anthology of His Works*, ed., O. Manthey-Zorn (New York: Washington Square Press, 1964), p. 120.
2. Jn. 3:3
3. For proof that some very unstable people may profit under proper supervision see the account of the work of Grof with psychotics in this volume, chapter 7.
4. More specific information has been given in the last section of chapter 8.
5. See S. H. Thompson, *Hell's Angels* (New York: Ballantine Books, 1961); J. R. Allen and L. J. West, "The Flight from Violence: Hippies and the Green Rebellion," *American Journal of Psychiatry*, 125, no. 3 (Sept., 1965), pp. 364-370.
6. Robert E. L. and Jean Houston Masters of the Foundation for Mind

Research in New York, are experimenting with mechanical means of producing ecstasy.

7. E. L. Sostrom "Group Therapy; Let the Buyer Beware," *Psychology Today* 2, no. 9 (Feb., 1969).

8. Nietzsche, *Anthology*, p. 120.

9. A model of such combination of criticism and understanding is to be found in J. Havens, "A Working Paper: Memo on the Implications of the Consciousness-Changing Drugs," *Journal for the Scientific Study of Religion*, 3, no. 2 (Spring, 1964), pp. 216-226, or "A Memo to Quakers on the Consciousness-Changing Drugs," mimeographed and procurable from Dr. Joseph Havens, Counseling Services, Univ. of Massachusetts, Amherst.

Selected References

Abramson, H. A., ed. *The Use of LSD in Psychotherapy and Alcoholism*. (Bobbs, Merrill, 1967). Authoritative articles by world experts.

Alpert, R., Cohen, S. & Shiller, L. *LSD*. (New American Library, 1966—paper). Contrasting views of two experts: Alpert, a supporter of the religious and other uses of LSD; Cohen, much nearer the position of the medical establishment.

Blum, R. & Associates. *Utopiates: the Use and Users of LSD-25*. (Atherton, 1965). Chapter by Downing & Wygant a good consideration of religion.

Braden, Wm. *The Private Sea: LSD and the Search for God* (Quadrangle Books, 1967). A very competent reporter approaches the subject theologically and comparatively.

Clark, W. H. "Religion and the Consciousness Expanding Substances," in E. P. Booth, ed. *Religion Ponders Science* (Appleton-Century, 1964). In part an account of a self-experiment.

Cohen, S. "Lysergic Acid Diethylamide: Side Effects and Complications," in *Journal of Nervous and Mental Disease* (January, 1960). Most comprehensive study so far of harmful mental side effects with incidence in both normals and patients—25,000 ingestions.

Crockett, Sandison, and Walk, eds. *Hallucinogenic Drugs and Their Psychotherapeutic Use* (Chas. C. Thomas, 1963). Proceedings of a Royal Medico-Psychological Association colloquium in England with distinguished worldwide participation.

deRopp, R. S. *Drugs and the Mind* (Grove—paper, 1960). A popular presentation by a former Rockefeller Foundation biochemist includes information on psychedelics.

Dunlap, Jane. *Exploring Inner Space* (Harcourt, Brace, 1961—also in paper). A journalist describes her experience as a patient.

167

Havens, Jos. "Memo on the Consciousness-Expanding Drugs," in *Journal for the Scientific Study of Religion* (Spring, 1964). A searching and thorough commentary based on the author's experience.

Huxley, A. *The Doors of Perception* (Harper—paper, 1963). Huxley's famous self-experiment, with other material.

James, Wm. *The Varieties of Religious Experience* (Various editions, including paper). The classical work on the psychology of religion: stimulating, religiously penetrating, well written. The Lecture on Mysticism describes James' self-experiments with drugs.

Jordan, G. Ray, Jr. "LSD and Mystical Experience," in *Journal of Bible and Religion* (April, 1963). Perceptive firsthand account.

Leary, T. *High Priest* (World Publishing Company, 1968). An amazingly frank account of experiences with and reactions to the psychedelics up to, but not including, his expulsion from Harvard; an important document, very readable.

———. *The Politics of Ecstasy* (G. P. Putnam's Sons, 1968). A rather miscellaneous collection of papers and addresses but provocative, controversial, satirical and perceptive; basically a religious commentary on morals, psychotherapy and culture.

Masters, R. E. M. & Houston, J. *The Varieties of Psychedelic Experience*. (Holt, Rinehart, and Winston, 1966). A readable, knowledgeable and full survey of psychedelic phenomena, probably the best available.

Metzner, R., ed. *The Ecstatic Adventure* (Macmillan, 1968). A well edited collection of firsthand accounts of chemical ecstasy.

Murry, G. B., S.J. "Pharmacological Mysticism" in *Revue de l'Université d'Ottawa* (April-June, 1968). Informed account by a Catholic scientist.

Pahnke, W. N. "Drugs and Mysticism: an Analysis of the Relationship Between Psychedelic Drugs and Mystical Consciousness" (Harvard Ph.D. Dissertation, 1964). The full account of the Good Friday experiment summarized by Pahnke & Richards in *Journal of Religion and Health* (July, 1966); also see chapter by Pahnke in Abramson volume.

Psychedelic Information Center Bulletin (Editor, Lisa Bieberman, 26 Boylston Street, #3, Cambridge, Mass. 02138). This ably and brightly edited sheet published every two months is one of the best means of keeping up to date on developments. Not sold, but send self-addressed, stamped envelope for each current number. For example, #22 (Feb., 1969) surveys evidence on chromosomal and genetic damage thought to be possible with LSD; #24 (June, 1969) surveys state laws regarding psychedelic drugs. Issues in print (from about #12 on) are available at 10¢ an issue along with other material.

Slotkin, J. S. *The Peyote Religion* (Free Press—paper, 1956). Most concise account of Native American Church by an anthropologist.

Solomon, D. E. ed. *LSD: the Consciousness-Expanding Drug* (Putnam's, 1964). Excellent articles on both sides of the controversy.

Stace, W. T. *Mysticism and Philosophy* (Lippincott, 1960). Excellent treatise on mysticism by Princeton's expert; deals with drugs in chap. 1.

Stafford, P. G. & Golightly, B. H. *LSD: the Problem-Solving Psychedelic* (Award Books—paper, 1967). Accurate journalistic summary of constructive uses of the drugs; full annotated bibliography.

Unger, S. M. "Mescaline, LSD, Psilocybin, and Personality Change" in *Psychiatry* (May, 1963). Full review of research literature to 1963; for the scholar.

Zaehner, R. C. *Mysticism: Sacred and Profane* (Oxford: Clarendon Press, 1957). Among other things, an Oxford scholar, who has tried mescaline, holds that drugs do not induce truly religious mysticism.

Films. Most films in this field are propagandistic and nondiscriminating attempts to warn youth against using drugs. One of the best documentaries is the 50-minute film, "The Spring Grove Experiment" on the use of LSD in psychotherapy. McGraw-Hill Book Co., 330 W. 42nd St., N.Y.C. 10036, will send list of rental libraries making it available.

Taking the Drugs. It would be surprising if there were not some readers of this book desiring to take the drugs under careful conditions. Failing the unlikely opportunity to volunteer as a subject in a properly sanctioned experiment, the only legal alternative in North America is to apply to the Hollywood Hospital, New Westminster, B.C., near Vancouver. For a fee between $400 and $500, and subject to screening, anyone can be given the drugs under expert care. Preliminary screening can be done by mail. Most will find the trip worth the expense.

Psychedelics can be administered by experts in several European countries, notably Czechoslovakia.

Index

171